IMAGINING

OURSELVES

GLOBAL VOICES FROM A NEW GENERATION OF WOMEN

IMAGINING OURSELVES

EDITOR
Paula Goldman

ASSOCIATE EDITOR
Hafsat Abiola

FOREWORD BY
Isabel Allende

PUBLISHED IN ASSOCIATION WITH
INTERNATIONAL™
MUSEUM OF WOMEN

NEW WORLD LIBRARY
NOVATO, CALIFORNIA

To my parents, Michele and Milton Goldman, for generosity beyond words.

And to Denise Dunning, for knowing in her bones that anything, really, truly, is possible.

PAULA GOLDMAN

New World Library
14 Pamaron Way
Novato, CA 94949

For photo credits and permissions acknowledgments, see page 238.

Cover design, text design, and typography by Debbie Berne, Herter Studio, San Francisco / www.herterstudio.com

First printing, March 2006
ISBN-10: 1-57731-524-3
ISBN-13: 978-157731-524-7
Printed in Hong Kong on acid-free paper

Distributed by Publishers Group West

10 9 8 7 6 5 4 3 2 1

Library of Congress Cataloging-in-Publication Data

Imagining ourselves : global voices from a new generation of women / Paula Goldman, editor ; Hafsat Abiola, associate editor ; foreword by Isabel Allende.
   p. cm.
   "Published in association with the International Museum of Women."
   Includes bibliographical references.
   ISBN 1-57731-524-3 (pbk. : alk. paper)
 1. Women—Social conditions—21st century. 2. Young women—Social conditions—21st century. 3. Young women—Cross-cultural studies. 4. Young women—Biography. I. Goldman, Paula. II. Abiola, Hafsat. III. International Museum of Women.
   HQ1155.I63 2005
   305.242'2'0905II—dc22

   2005022617

PAGES 3–4 BETTINA SALOMON • AUSTRIA / *Feeling Alive*   PAGES 7–8 MEHRANEH ATASHI • IRAN / *Collage*
[For Bettina Salomon's bio, see page 201. For Mehraneh Atashi's bio, see page 238.]

CONTENTS

[CONTRIBUTORS]

[AN INVITATION TO READERS]

YOU'RE PROBABLY WONDERING WHAT THIS BOOK IS ABOUT, and further, why a museum might be involved. This book is an important part of a larger project that starts a conversation — one that we want you to join, one that we are convinced holds the possibility of positively changing your life and the world. This conversation will bring you together with your peers in every corner of the world — from Beijing to Bogotá, San Francisco to Saint Petersburg, Cairo to Calcutta — to talk about the experiences and goals that unite young women across national boundaries, across cultures, and across backgrounds.

The power and potential of today's global generation of women in their twenties and thirties is enormous. The Imagining Ourselves project creates a platform that spotlights the extraordinary contributions of these young women to their families, communities, economies, and societies. It aims to unite young women through dialogue and ultimately inspire them to action.

For precisely this reason and more, the International Museum of Women proudly and boldly chose this project, and the generation of women in their twenties and thirties around the world, to invest in. We believe that the project aligns beautifully with the International Museum of Women's vision of equity for all.

In the pages of this book, you'll find many beautiful photographs and paintings, as well as amazing personal stories and powerful poems. But it is more than just an art book. It is a portrait of a generation, featuring the best of thousands of submissions from young women across the globe in response to the question, *What defines your generation of women?* The contributors include many well-known artists, athletes, and leaders, and all of the pieces are thoughtful and provocative.

The Imagining Ourselves project combines this inspiring anthology with an online exhibit and gathering place where you can participate in conversations about topics important to you. The conversation begins on International Women's Day, March 8, 2006, and will last until June 30, 2006, at the International Museum of Women's website, www.imow.org. We invite you to contribute your unique experiences and perspective, as well as your energy, humor, and courageous spirit, to become part of a global community of young women whose leadership will transform the world as we know it.

When you and your peers read about each other's hopes, fears, and bold moves to contribute positively to your communities, engage in conversation that matters to you, and unite to tackle the challenges and opportunities important to your generation, you can help overcome the obstacles that women and girls face across the globe. You can form a future that allows you and your peers, as well as generations to come, to live your lives fully and find the freedom to create your own destinies. Of course, not all of today's women live in a world of abundant opportunities, but this project offers an opportunity, now, to work together to create that world for all.

We are counting on you and believe in you — and we know that our vision would not be complete without you. Come, join the conversation!

CHRIS YELTON
PRESIDENT, INTERNATIONAL MUSEUM OF WOMEN

GATHER THE

[FOREWORD]

BY ISABEL ALLENDE

WOMEN

When I was growing up in the 1950s in Chile, girls were not supposed to mingle with boys. Swimming in the same pool with a male might get an honest girl pregnant, not to mention what might come of holding hands in the darkness of a movie theater or slow dancing. We were raised to follow in our mothers' footsteps. Ideally, we would ignore any personal ambition, control anger, repress imagination, and deny sexuality. Good manners were essential, and one should be careful not to outsmart men if one wanted to lure a husband. I had no raw material to be a lady, so I rebelled as soon as I realized that being born a female was not exactly to my advantage: it would take double the effort to get half the recognition and respect that any male got. Did I want to be a man? Of course! But it was not Freudian envy, please. Why would I envy that unreliable little organ? I simply wanted to have the same freedom and advantages that my brothers enjoyed.

When I was in my teens the birth control pill was invented, and suddenly everything changed for women. It took a while for the concept of strong, empowered women to reach Chile, and even longer to reach my neolithic family, but eventually it did. I still remember my astonishment when I read *The Female Eunuch* by Germaine Greer and other books by female writers of the 1960s and 1970s. I discovered that there was an articulate and humorous language to the fight for women's rights. Soon I started working as a journalist with a women's magazine. We were five young women who dared to tackle the issues that no one discussed in public. I am proud to say that in a few years we made dramatic changes in our culture. Wow, did we get a lot of aggression! But it was fun. Every minute was worth it.

Amazingly, most of the aggression towards us did not come from men but from other women who felt threatened. Change is always scary. Trying to protect me, my mother advised me often not to confront the establishment. Instead, she said, I had to learn to manipulate it. That's what women had always done, why couldn't I do the same? And what about my family? Children needed a full-time mother; it was a biological obligation, wasn't it? These questions would seem almost a joke to many young women today, but they created a feeling of guilt — even shame — in me and other young women who had decided to pursue a career. Was something basically wrong with us? Doubts were always in the back of our minds, but we kept on pushing our beliefs. Fortunately we had each other.

In my case I also had two guardian angels — an adopted grandmother and my mother-in-law — who helped raise my kids while I juggled three jobs. And I had an understanding husband. He did not stand in my way, and for that I am grateful, but he didn't share any of the domestic chores. Maintaining the household and raising the kids were my responsibilities alone. One had to be a superwoman to cope with that life.

The obstacles seemed immense to the women of my generation, but so was our energy. The first lesson we learned was that we were not alone in our ideals, and sharing them gave us incredible strength. We were convinced that we would win the war, even if we lost a few battles, and in due time — fifteen or twenty years at the most — women all over would have much better lives. We wanted all our sisters to feel the power that we felt. We urged them to pursue their dreams, to be in control of their lives, to get together and support each other. Our motto was "Gather the women, and they will change the world!"

More than thirty years have passed. In my lifetime I have seen many positive changes, but not enough. The world that my granddaughters will inherit is certainly a better place than the one I was born into, but not for all women, only for those who are educated. The rest have hard lives. Girls in some places are still sold into early marriage, prostitution, and labor; women are forced to have children they can't support; they are abused, raped, even killed with impunity. In most societies women are the poorest of the poor. In times of war they are the first victims, just as they are the first targets of religious fundamentalism.

Seeing how much still needs to be done, sometimes I get depressed.

But then one day this project, *Imagining Ourselves,* landed on my desk. It rapidly turned my discouragement into joy. Here was what I had been hoping for, for years! The world is filled with fierce girls who do not question their power, who feel that they can do anything, who have never contemplated their limitations, only their possibilities. This would have been unthinkable thirty years ago. Women's issues today are less overtly political and more personal than they were before, but they are alive. Now it is less about denouncing, protesting, and fighting and more about setting positive goals and encouraging creativity among women. We have come a long way, baby!

When Paula Goldman, the young editor of *Imagining Ourselves,* set out to find out how her peers feel today, she was not expecting the response she got. Three thousand women in 105 countries answered her call. This astounding book is the result of that search. If I ever was discouraged by the limited gains made by women, this book gave me back the passionate optimism of my youth. I am startled by the assured attitude of these young women, their creative force, and their capacity for leadership. They feel that the future is wide open to them. They know that they are not alone and that millions of others are examining and dealing with the same predicaments. Nothing can stop them.

This young generation of women will have a tremendous impact on the future; it will change our civilization and lead us to another stage of evolution. Even if not all women have achieved everything that my generation wished for them, one thing is true: never before in history have so many women felt so empowered. The dream of gathering the women has come true. And this is excellent news!

INTRODUCTION

BY PAULA GOLDMAN

The Imagining Ourselves project began in the fall of 2001, during a casual breakfast conversation with a friend. I was twenty-six years old, freshly minted with a master's degree in public policy, full of dreams about making a difference in the world...but jobless, broke, and utterly lost.

The timing of the initiation of my career could not have been worse. The economy was awful, and September 11 had just happened. I'd given up a fellowship to go to Israel and Palestine to write a book about peacemaking in the region because I feared for my physical safety there — and because peace seemed like a naïve dream. For lack of a better plan, I grudgingly moved back home with my parents and started looking for a job in dot-com-bust San Francisco. I wanted desperately to do meaningful work, but getting any kind of work whatsoever was a challenge. I spent days sitting in the backyard, smoking cigarettes I didn't even enjoy, dreading my parents' nightly return when they would ask me if I'd made any progress with the job search.

One Sunday, Denise Dunning, a friend from graduate school who had also moved out to the Bay Area, invited me over for breakfast. We started the morning discussing the usual topics: dating and gossip about mutual friends. But somehow our conversation drifted into recounting the stories of young women we knew all around the world and the incredible things they were up to. Both Denise and I had worked and traveled in numerous countries, and each of us knew dozens of incredible women around our age who were making courageous moves in their lives and contributing vital leadership to their communities. Many had started their own nonprofit organizations or were quickly climbing the corporate ladder. Others had made exciting innovations in the art world or were charting new ground in their families or personal lives.

It dawned on us that there was something quite remarkable that connected all of these stories — a positive, empowered spirit that enabled women of our generation to engage fully with the world and to pursue goals and lifestyles that may not have been possible several decades ago. But why had this experience not been recognized or presented to the world at large? How could we publicly convey the sheer energy and beauty of our peers in a way that moved beyond old stereotypes?

"What about an anthology?" I asked Denise casually, not really even moved by my own idea. To my surprise, she responded enthusiastically and volunteered to help.

Like all of life's best adventures, if I had known what I was getting into, I never would have started. Luckily, I had no clue. I thought the book would take about a year from start to finish. Nearly five years and thousands of conversations later, the journey is still just beginning.

● ● ●

It started small. I gathered a few local friends and composed a short call for submissions, asking women to send in artwork and writings that responded to the question, *What defines your generation of women?* We sent it out by email through a few organizations working internationally, but it didn't take long to figure out that our approach wouldn't cut it.

Consider this: there are more than one billion women between the ages of twenty and forty located in more than 193 countries speaking more than six thousand languages. If we wanted to reach even a fraction of them, we had to get serious. We approached the International Museum of Women and asked them to partner with us on the project. We had nothing more than a good idea, but they believed in us enough to generously put their name behind the project, to offer practical advice and moral support, and to give us the office infrastructure to get started.

Next, we formed an international advisory committee of more than twenty-five women from around the world who helped us translate our call into multiple languages and distribute it through hundreds of grassroots networks. Week one: universities around the world; week two: art groups; and so on, for nearly six months, until my entire team wanted to kill me.

We feared we wouldn't get any reaction, but the response was overwhelming: more than three thousand replies from around the globe and close to eight hundred formal submissions from 105 countries. Significantly, 90 percent of the submissions came in by email, which would not have been possible even five years earlier, before the rapid global proliferation of this technology in the late 1990s.

More inspiring than the sheer number of responses was the quality of the content itself. We began the project with an intuition about the wonderful things that young adult women were up to, but the bold, inspired responses we received exceeded our wildest expectations.

• • •

If you are a woman between the ages of twenty and forty living anywhere on the globe today, you are part of the most educated, most well-traveled, most professionally empowered, most international generation of women ever to have existed on this planet. It's a story that not many people are telling yet, but it's one of the most inspiring stories out there in a world full of violence and insecurity — the story of a generation of women poised to take the reins of global leadership like no other generation in history.

As you will read in part 2 of this book, more young women today have had access to formal education than at any other time in history. Literacy rates for women increased dramatically in the eighties and nineties, and more women work today than ever before. This is also a generation that is increasingly connected across national boundaries. As the gender gap in Internet access quickly closes (at last count, 51 percent of Internet users in the United States and 49 percent in countries like South Africa were women),[1] many of us use the Web to keep up with friends and news from different continents. International travel is on the rise too. Young women, especially in places like the former Soviet Union and large parts of East Asia, are using their newfound mobility, both financial and political, to tour and experience large parts of the world.

Does this include everyone? Does every young woman enjoy such privileges as travel and professional freedom? Could every young woman in the world have received our email calling for participation in a global dialogue? Of course not. Less than 15 percent of the world's population has Internet access, and most of those who do live in the West.[2] Globally, women and girls still comprise 70 percent of people living in poverty.[3] Problems such as human trafficking and domestic violence are as serious for women today as they have ever been, or perhaps more so.

It is crucial to acknowledge that the perspectives offered in this book are mostly those of women who have benefited from demographic shifts over the last few decades. By and large, they are the voices of women who are in the middle or upper-middle classes of their countries, women who have had access to education and technology; they are not the voices of the poor and underprivileged. But they *are* voices that represent a growing segment of our generation. And they *are* voices that represent an incredibly significant moment in the history of women's lives, a moment that deserves to be recognized and celebrated.

Because to miss the wonder of our generation's experience is to miss what many of our mothers and grandmothers and great-grandmothers (and many of their husbands and lovers and friends) worked so hard for. To deny the breadth and significance of the privileges that so many young women enjoy is to deny that *dreams of creating positive change in the world can indeed come true,* even if they take a long time and don't look the way you initially expected them to look.

It is precisely this message that filtered through when our team took a close look at the overwhelming amount of material we had collected in response to our call for submissions. Self-assuredness rang in the voices of so many young women — and conviction that anything was possible. Whether in the arena of self-expression or professional achievement, whether in negotiating one's identity as an immigrant or in reflecting on being a new mother, there was this utterly uplifting, seductive, funny, *kick-ass* spirit that united all of the women with whom we were in contact.

It was the voice of Erika Hibbert, who spoke about young women in South

Africa mending the collective wounds of apartheid. It was the voice of Jessica Loseby from England, who talked about successfully having a family despite being confined to a wheelchair — something that would have been virtually unthinkable for a disabled woman even a generation ago. It was the voice of Mayerly Sánchez, who, in the midst of Colombia's civil war, had the idea to organize youth against the violence — and she did. She orchestrated a historic national vote in which thousands of kids and teenagers across the country went to the polls to make a highly televised statement against the violence. And one month later, as a result, tens of thousands of adult Colombians also went to the polls to demand an end to forced kidnapping and abuses of children associated with the war.

Mayerly did not grow up as an elite member of her society. She did not have access to extraordinary wealth or networks of privilege. She, like so many of the participants in this project, was simply a young woman with a good idea who did not stop to question the proposition that she could make a difference in the world.

How exciting to bring all these people together, to amplify the power of their confidence and humor! How much momentum might come from this interchange of ideas and experiences!

From there, work on this project progressed naturally. We created an international committee to select the works that were to appear in this book — striving for both diversity of ideas and aesthetic quality. Instead of aiming narrowly to have one young woman represented from every country in the world, we aimed for relative parity of representation from all major geographic regions. We chose some entries because they inspired us, some because they reminded us of the challenges young women face, and others that were controversial because they provoked us and made us think.

We then began to strategize about using the Internet as a platform for global participation in this project — so we could reach people who couldn't afford to buy a nice book in a bookstore. We started crafting educational outreach programs to get these stories into universities and secondary schools. And so on.

• • •

Every so often I look back at what's become of a casual breakfast conversation, and I am astounded. With a tentative question, *How do we capture the spirit of our generation?* we inspired the thousands of women (and one man!) who answered our call for submissions, the tens of thousands of people who read or helped distribute our inquiry to the world's young women, and the hundreds of thousands of people who will continue the effort to create a vision for the future of women by participating in our online exhibit and global gathering.

One small idea sent ripples all across this planet of ours. And in the process, my own life has also been permanently transformed. I remember when we first started asking prominent young women to participate in *Imagining Ourselves.* Zadie Smith was in town to give a reading from her novel, and I stood in line afterward like a dormouse, waiting to ask her to be a contributor to our book. When I got to the front of the line, I was so self-conscious that I barely managed to spit out a few coherent sentences, and given my delivery, I'm still not sure why she said yes. Today, I don't think twice about voicing what I think is important, not to anyone, be they a head of state or a Nobel Laureate, and indeed, such opportunities are now available. I didn't even know this kind of self-assurance was possible five years ago.

None of this, of course, was smooth sailing. I can't count the number of conversations in which a potential collaborator or donor gave us a blank stare and just did not get why we thought this was important. I can't count the number of times I called my poor parents, wanting to throw in the towel, feeling like I must be crazy for investing so much of myself in a project that seemed like it would never pan out. In the end, what got me through those rough patches was a little voice inside my head that told me this really was achievable. It just required an unseemly amount of persistence. And, of course, a healthy sense of humor.

The other day, I was flipping through my journal from that blue time of 2001, and I was stunned to find a stream-of-consciousness scribble that predicted exactly this outcome — the one I want so badly not just for me but also for you, for all of us:

> And. you. will.
> walk across rivers so wide, so high
> so deep with abundant joy
>
> that your eyes will dart back
> in wonder. How did i ever get here,
> to this place. How.
>
> and how could i
> ever have lived otherwise.
>
> That life i dreamed.
> was not a life. that churning in my stomach
> was not my soul. but a creative,
> dumbfounded little girl, struggling
> to speak.

• • •

We have the power to move the world, each and every one of us. If you are a woman in your twenties or thirties, it is likely that you have access to more resources to transform your life, and the lives of those around you, than any woman of a previous generation in history.

More than anything, I hope that this book will remind you how much is possible, how much impact you can have on the world just by having a good idea and following through with it, despite the obstacles you may find in your path. I hope that as you flip through these pages, you will be inspired by the visions and actions of your peers throughout the world. You might even walk away with ideas for new projects — or entirely new directions for your life.

Most important, I invite you to take some time to consider how you can make a difference in the lives of other young women (and men!). What can you do to benefit members of our generation who do not have access to the same luxuries you do — who may never have a chance to read a book like this or hear the wisdom of their peers from around the world? How can you make the most of the opportunities you've been granted so that others may also have similar ones?

Chances are you're already thinking about some of these questions. So when you're out there taking a big risk in your life, remember that hundreds of thousands of other young women across the globe are taking similar risks. And when you're out there being a leader in your community, at your office, or in your family, remember that your actions are significant, even when they don't seem to be — *especially* when they don't seem to be.

The victories you achieve in your own life make similar ones possible for all of us.

•   •   •

What would happen if we thought of ourselves as the recipients of a legacy? Today we enjoy countless privileges inherited from the efforts of innumerable generations before our own. And today we are grown; we are young women from a generation preparing to influence and illuminate this world.

We have the opportunity to create a new conversation with our ideas, thoughts, passions, and skills — one that is based not just on the problems facing women but on our joy, confidence, and spirit as well.

Today we decide what we want, and nothing is impossible.

INSIDE >>

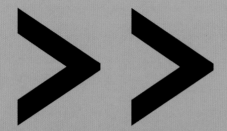

EVERY SO OFTEN, we catch a glimpse of ourselves.

Maybe the moment comes in a quiet conversation with a friend or as we look in the mirror to check how we are dressed. Most days, we glance quickly at our reflection before rushing off to start the day. But once in a rare while, we take a moment to notice the woman staring back at us, to notice all the things going on internally that may not be visible to the outside world.

Who is it that we see?

The entries in this chapter are answers to that question; they are intimate portraits of young women coming to terms with who they are and consciously deciding who they want to become. As a generation, young women are getting (and taking!) more and more time for such explorations, a luxury that goes hand in hand with changing demographics.

Over the past few decades, the shifts have been dramatic. In countries where women were getting married in their early and mid-twenties, they are now doing so in their mid-twenties and early thirties; where they were wedding in their teens, they are now doing so in their early twenties. And as women participate in formal education and in the paid workforce in greater numbers (a subject that figures prominently in part 2), they are also delaying motherhood and having fewer children. These changes immediately affect our day-to-day lives as we pass through our twenties and thirties, arguably creating more space for conscious reflection and questioning.

We begin part 1 with a discussion of spirituality, one of the most powerful tools for unlocking and understanding the depths of our experiences. As the global economy moves forward at breakneck speed, many young women are actually reinventing their own relationships to spirituality and religion, finding creative ways to honor the traditions of their ancestors and make them relevant to contemporary life. Anila Umar, a Canadian whose parents are from India and Pakistan, finds strength in her Islamic heritage by reclaiming the notion of jihad as valiant personal struggle and journey rather than as a form of extremist violence, as it is sometimes invoked in Western media. Yen Chua, a prominent Singaporean painter, professes to have discovered her spiritual self while on a trek through the Himalayas. She now creates exquisite, Buddhist-inspired paintings, cultivating a sense of peace and connectedness with nature amid the hustle and bustle of urban life.

Few things are more intimate than our relationship with our body, so it is no surprise that we received enough submissions about beauty and self-image to merit their own section in this chapter. Some of these pieces have a serious tone. For example, Toyin Sokefun and Yemisi Nzan Ogbe tell us how beauty pageants in Nigeria create unrealistic standards for appearance to which the average Nigerian woman cannot (and does not wish to) measure up. But other young women demonstrate a decidedly playful approach in their attitudes towards beauty. Jessica Lagunas, an artist with roots in Nicaragua, Chile, and Guatemala, portrays herself putting on lipstick and nail polish in humorously exaggerated ways. And the photographs of Fakhriya Al-Yahyai reveal beautiful fabrics and textures of women's clothing in her native Oman details that are usually hidden from view under a black gown. These pieces are positive and fun, allowing room for the joy and satisfaction that so many women share in the ritual of getting dressed up and looking good.

Next, we address our personal relationships with others. How are young women exploring the changing nature of romance in an age when marriage and family are being continually redefined? Shen Ling, a Chinese painter, shows us how young women in Beijing are revamping traditional roles with respect to dating, learning how to value (and achieve) their own satisfaction in romantic situations. Lada Karitskaya's beautiful short story narrates the tale of a young Russian woman who ultimately decides not to go on a date with an American suitor... whom she met on the Internet! On the flip side, Jolivette Mecenas, a Filipina American, chimes in with a humorous piece about how to navigate the funny looks young single women sometimes get from waiters and other diners when they dare to eat alone at a fine restaurant. Jolivette's piece reminds us of the ways our generation continues to carve out spaces for alternative lifestyles, whether that means choosing to be single, living with a same-sex partner, or raising children on our own.

Perhaps most inspirational is the last set of entries, which focus more broadly on personal reflection and self-development. Our twenties and thirties can be pivotal years. For some of us, they are a time when childhood goals are exposed to the world to be tested and remade, and for others, they are the years in which we come more fully into our own. They can encompass both great discoveries and times of challenge, from the indescribable wonder of motherhood (as described by Israeli singer Achinoam Nini) to the despair of waking up at thirty and realizing that having a high-powered career may not be all there is to life (as described by novelist Lucía Etxebarría of Spain). Marcela Nievas, an Argentinean Australian, spends her twenties traveling to the ends of the earth, collecting colorful experiences and defining who she is in the world in relation to her surroundings. By contrast, Korean American poet Ishle Yi Park finds herself emerging in the actions she takes to defend her loved ones against the negative effects of poverty and violence.

At the end of the day, what Ishle discovers in herself now that her childhood struggles are over are the same qualities that unite so many young women today: an enduring strength, an enchanting humor, and the determination to create a life worthy of the new opportunities that have been presented to us.

FACTS & TRENDS

>> Globally, the average age of women at first marriage in 1970 was 21.4. By 2000 it had risen to 25.5.[1]

>> Since young people must meet ever-higher criteria (including more schooling) in order to become successful adults in the information age, the ladders they must climb to reach adulthood are lengthening. One study estimates that adolescents in rural India, for example, are now considered to be adults at the age of sixteen rather than twelve. In postindustrial societies like the United States, the age has shifted from twenty-two to twenty-six.[2]

>> The global cosmetics and toiletries market was valued at $201 billion in 2003. Together, the United States and Japan represent a third of worldwide sales. Latin America also holds a significant share of the market, comprising 9.3 percent of sales. The cosmetics markets in Russia and large parts of East Asia are strong — and growing — as well.[3]

>> In the 1980s, when researchers asked young women in Peru how many children they wanted to have, the average answer was 3.8. Just one decade later, in the 1990s, that number had dropped to 2.5. In the 1980s in Egypt, women desired 4.1 children, but by the 1990s they desired only 2.9.[4]

>> In the West and in former Soviet regions, births outside formal marriage have become more common. In Bulgaria in 1990, 12 percent of births were to unwed mothers, and from 1994 to 1998, 30 percent were. In Norway in 1990, 39 percent of births were to unwed mothers, and by 1994, 49 percent were.[5]

>> In almost all Western and former Soviet countries, the birth rate is now below the replacement level.[6]

SPIRIT

ANNA RIKKINEN · FINLAND

Anna Rikkinen, born in 1976 in Asikkala, Finland, grew up under the guidance of three generations of women. Her passion for body-related objects began with her jewelry studies in Amsterdam. Inspired by the flirtatious qualities of jewelry and historical clothing, she works with concepts of beauty and the matters of attraction and defense, covering and revealing.

LEFT *Angel*

I am a young African American female painter married to a white male who is pursuing a career in emergency medicine. My relationship itself is a possibility that was open to me that was not accepted in my mother's or grandmother's generation. I feel that although some people still don't like the idea of interracial relationships, it is more accepted now, especially among people of my generation.

I describe my work as urban folklore. The images meld contemporary African American urban culture and history with traditional African culture. All of these creations are centered on an individual's journey to Sivad. In my work, Sivad represents not only a fictitious urban village to which people travel physically, but an internal, spiritual journey to reach a higher consciousness. Each painting reflects an essential moment in an individual's journey. Ancestor spirits, represented by blue figures or blue light, help guide these people as they travel day to day in search of Sivad.

My work is inspired by the stories of people around me — whether it is what I saw when my eyes briefly connected with those of an old woman while walking down Mission Street or the feeling I got when I talked to a single mother struggling to raise three children. I feel that

a story should never be owned by just one person, but rather experienced by many. Storytelling has been defined as an oral tradition, folklore passed on through generations of people through speech, by the "tellers." In the tradition of an African griot, I pass on the stories of everyday people. Rather than telling the stories verbally, I am sharing them visually — on canvas. I want these stories to be available to my generation as well as generations to come. These stories deserve a place in history too.

KEINA DAVIS ELSWICK • USA

Keina Davis Elswick has been painting since she was seven years old. Early on, she made a promise to herself that she would be able to support herself with her art by age thirty. Despite doubts and fears expressed by friends and teachers who thought she would become a starving artist, she reports achieving this goal by age twenty-six. A graduate of the University of Florida, Keina currently lives in San Francisco with her husband, Benjamin.

LEFT *In the Eyes of Faith*

REGAN BALZER • NEW ZEALAND

Regan Balzer, born in 1975, is a painter and the mother of two children. She teaches art, design, and mathematics part-time at a local Kura Kaupapa Mäori (a type of Mäori middle school) and at various times to adults. The motivating force behind her work is *nga matauranga Mäori* (Mäori knowledge) and its application to life in a contemporary world.

ABOVE *Nga Hine Tuatahi (The First Woman)*

This painting depicts the first women of the world. In Mäori tradition, Hineahuone was the first person. She was molded by the *atua* (god) Tane from the clay of the earth mother, Papatuanuku. Once her form was finished, each *atua* gifted an element towards her creation.

This traditional story explains our connections to the earth, each other, and the divine. We are losing many of our people to drugs, violence, alcohol, and lost self-worth. This narrative reminds us that we are all special. We all have gifts that have been handed down through the generations from our ancestors. Our ancestors are us, and we are them.

Let us all remember.

Personal Jihad: The Struggle Within

I have chosen a series of photographs I took in February 2003 while on hajj, the Muslim pilgrimage to Mecca, to answer the question, What defines your generation of women? First, let me begin with a brief explanation. Followers of the religion of Islam are grounded by their faith and obedience in submission to what are known as the Five Pillars of Islam. These include (1) believing that there is no god but Allah and that Muhammad is His messenger, (2) praying five times daily, (3) fasting during the month of Ramadan, (4) giving alms to charity, and (5) making a pilgrimage, known as hajj, to the Muslim holy city of Mecca once in a person's lifetime.

Second, let me tell you about the Arabic word *jihad*. It has been thrown around a lot in the media, and therefore many people now believe that *jihad* means "holy war" and is an excuse for Muslims to become violent. Fighting for one's religion or belief system, as in a holy war, would be a type of jihad, yes, but that is not the only or even the most common use of the word. In fact, the word *jihad* simply means "struggle," and that is the meaning it holds for me and I hope for many other Muslims. As a young Muslim woman, I believe it refers to my personal struggle within myself.

I am a twenty-five-year-old Canadian woman. My parents are originally from India and Pakistan. It has been hard for me growing up in Canada. For years I was confused about my identity. Am I Canadian? Am I Indian? Am I Pakistani? Am I Muslim? I finally came to the conclusion that I am all of these and yet none of them. The only thing I really am is Anila — a young woman struggling within herself to personally effect change, a young woman who wants other young girls to grow up feeling less confused about who they are and proud of being themselves, not the statues that society creates, statues of perfect little girls who grow up to be perfect little women. I am a young woman who is struggling to gain inner peace, to reconcile who she is, within herself.

And I do not feel alone. In fact, I know that there are many women of my generation who are struggling with their own inner jihad. Why are we different from the women who came before us and those who will come after us? Because we are part of something unique in history. We are women who can no longer be boxed into one nationality because our families have moved. We are women who cannot be boxed into one race because our families have intermarried. We are women who cannot even be boxed into one religion because of our experiences. We are learning, we are changing, we are adapting, and we are accepting many different ways of thinking, behaving, and believing.

The series of photographs I have submitted take you on a step-by-step journey through the most important part of my personal jihad. I took the photographs at Jamarath in Saudi Arabia. At Jamarath, Muslims throw stones at a pillar that symbolizes the devil. It is the last rite we perform to complete our hajj. When we throw the rocks, we are letting all evil in the world know that we have completed hajj

The walk from Mina to Jamarath. My mother is to the left in a veil, and my father is directly in the center.

We approach the pillar.

and are now clean. We will no longer knowingly cause any evil in this world. We are letting the devil know that we have spent the last few days fighting him and we have won.

It was a turning point in my life when I walked all of the kilometers to Jamarath from Mina, where our camp was set up. We were an army of four million people who had sacrificed and struggled to make an oath that we would try to do only good in this world. We were no longer going to be pushed around by evil. We had each won a significant battle in our personal jihad. This was the most important day of my life because it solidified my beliefs. It was the day I realized that I am not alone and that being Anila is perfectly okay.

Throwing stones at the devil.

Throwing stones at the pillar.

ANILA UMAR • CANADA

While completing two college degrees — in biological sciences and psychology — Anila Umar also dedicated substantial time to advocating for the rights of immigrant and minority women and children in her hometown of Calgary, Alberta. For this work, and for her contribution to women's leadership and decision making, she received the 2001 Canadian Governor General's Award.

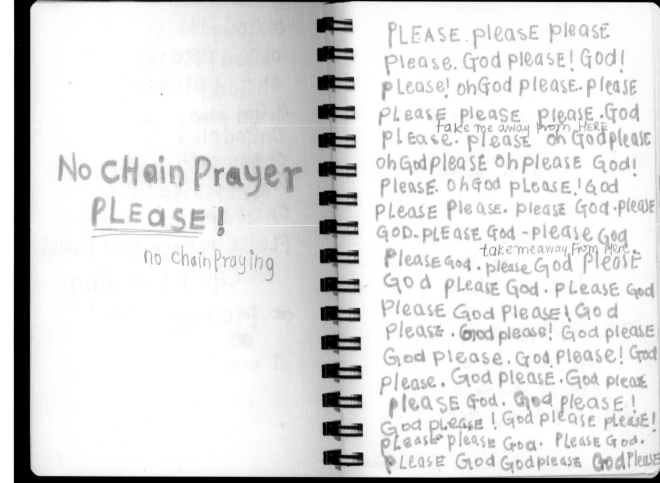

ABOVE *No Chain Praying Please*

SHIRIN KOULADJIE • IRAN

Shirin Kouladjie was born in Iran in 1965 and has since lived in various parts of the world, including Canada and the West Coast of the United States. Her keen interest in mathematics led her initially to a career in science, which was later supplanted by her creative desires as an artist. Shirin is a collector of sorts. She uses a broad sampling of popular media in her art, including newspaper clippings, wrappings, TV stills, and magazines.

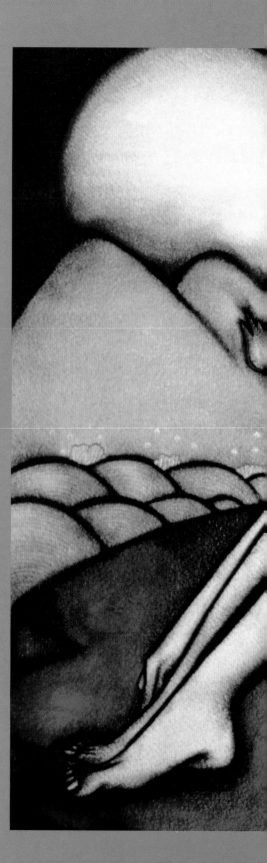

YEN CHUA • SINGAPORE

Yen Chua is a Singaporean artist whose work includes a collection of more than three hundred paintings, five solo exhibitions, and ten group exhibitions. In her recent journeys to Tibet and the Himalayan regions of Nepal and India, Yen discovered her spiritual self. Her works, heavily influenced by Buddhist traditions and precepts, illustrate her search for perfection in life and medium. Yen holds a bachelor of fine arts from the San Francisco Art Institute and a master of arts from the National Institute of Education in Singapore.

PREVIOUS PAGE *Taking Refuge II* RIGHT *Moon*

All the goddesses I am not

All the goddesses I am not
are gathered at my door.
It is an old rejection they come to reverse,
perverse and unbenign.
I do not let them in.
They are not like me.

Not Kali, the loudest,
clamoring for attention
the slow dance of skulls around her neck
bone music to my fears.
She is aggressive, that one,
and rude.
Look at the way she sticks out her tongue
at all who dare to look at her.
A red tongue, thirsty
for another demon to quench.
She drank his blood,
each self-perpetuating drop,
a furious suckling that saved the world.
Blood mother,
you would have killed us all.
It took a husband to make her stop
(Lord Shiva trembling
half-trampled beneath her feet),
and bite her tongue in shame.

Not Lakshmi, the meekest,
sprung perfectly beautiful
out of a tumultuous ocean of milk,

a lotus at her breast,
she, a lotus at the breast
of Vishnu, Lord Protector,
inseparable bride
gentle breathing light
riding her white owl
into the homes of the propitiary
casting dark glances and blight on those
who dare to slight her.
Mother of the world,
a whimsical tyrant,
feminine and full of wiles.

And not Durga, the fiercest.
A cosmic blaze of energy
in her eyes,
a pinwheel of mace and trident and sword.
Terrifying, but derived.
Free of husband, lord, or lover,
but formed fully of all their powers.
A sum total of gods then,
an essence of,
Shakti, distilled, concentrated,
burning the throat as it goes down.
Mother to none,
a lion between her thighs.

But
(and now I sense them listening, hushing,
pushing flat against the door)

SAMPURNA CHATTARJI · INDIA

Sampurna Chattarji was born in Dessie, Ethiopia, in 1970 and moved one year later with her family back to Darjeeling, India, where her father taught English at the Comprehensive School. After getting her bachelor's degree from Delhi University, she worked in advertising for five years in Calcutta, eventually quitting to pursue poetry and write full-time. She lives in Mumbai, India, with her husband, Kiran.

I have taken Kali's anger and made it mine.
My black moods are hers,
my irreverence.
I whoop, I rant, I rage.
Many hands girdle my waist.

I have swallowed Lakshmi whole.
She runs through me now,
a river of desire.
I drown myself and again,
I rise, a dreaming weed,
clinging to love, unworldly wise.

And Durga?
Durga has given me freedom,
and I have paid for it,
gladly.

She made a fighter of me.
She taught me when to raise my weapons,
screaming,
and when to lay my head in my mother's lap,
a daughter come home again.

I belong to a generation that has had the freedom to go against the grain. For me (as well as for many of my friends, all of whom share the same kind of elite, liberal education and come from similar middle-class backgrounds) forging a path that was markedly different from the one my mother took was an important way of defining myself. The further I moved away from the kind of woman my mother seemed to me, the closer I came to realizing how big a role she played in my self-definition. Only now do I realize how much she passed on to me of her subconscious disenchantment, her impatience with convention, her healthy disregard for the religious observances she learned from her own deeply devout mother but rejected for a more uncluttered approach to god.

Dichotomies, more than anything, define us, a group of women now in our early thirties — the keen edges of certainty a bit frayed, the first flush of triumphant rejections and personal successes fading down to introspection and reevaluation. We are being reclaimed by our mythologies, we are re-creating ourselves. For me, the Hindu goddesses I have never prayed to are my way of re-imagining myself.

BODY

HEBA FARID · EGYPT

Heba Farid was born in Cairo and has lived a life divided among three continents. She has a background in landscape architecture and earth sciences and is a multidisciplinary artist. One of her art projects focuses on reconstructing the life of her great-grandmother, Na'ima al-Misryya, a famous but forgotten female performer of early-twentieth-century Egypt.

LEFT From the *Unfolding Posture* series

JESSICA LAGUNAS • NICARAGUA

Born in Nicaragua to a Chilean father and Nicaraguan mother, Jessica Lagunas spent her childhood in Guatemala. In 2001 she and her husband went to New York City for a vacation, but they liked it so much that they decided to stay. A self-taught artist, Jessica has represented Guatemala in several international art festivals and makes a living as a graphic designer.

FACING PAGE *Para Acariciarte Mejor (In Order to Caress You Better)*
ABOVE *Para Besarte Mejor (In Order to Kiss You Better)*

One of the things that defines our generation of women in Nigeria, and in Lagos (the country's capital) in particular, is a conflicting self-image. We feel the need to live up to all of the different definitions of beauty offered by the legacy of generations of Nigerian women, cable television, the femme fatale in Nigerian men's heads, religious edicts, colonization, et cetera. We are torn between being ourselves and allowing others to determine who we are.

The photographs *Proud, Ouch!, Coy,* and *In the Eye of the Beholder* show different expressions of how women perceive themselves. The woman in *Proud,* for example, obviously views herself as beautiful, even if she is not the ideal, and the camera catches her in a very defiant mode. *In the Eye of the Beholder* shows a woman in her eighties who has settled into a natural view of her beauty, as can be deduced from her haircut. It is even possible that she is a widow; in most cases, elderly Nigerian widows are not encouraged to think of beauty. She is no longer compelled to fight, or to define herself in any way other than in relation to younger people, like her grandchildren and children. Unfortunately, her views on beauty and self-image are consequently not as relevant to our generation, but she represents what we may become. In essence, each of these photographs shows the absurdity of definitions of beauty.

TOYIN SOKEFUN • NIGERIA

Toyin Sokefun is a Nigerian artist who collaborated with her friend Yemizi Nzan Ogbe, a writer, to create *In the House of God,* a series of text and images on the theme of beauty. Toyin describes her photographs as representing her personal reflections on what true beauty is.

TOP LEFT *Proud* **TOP RIGHT** *Ouch!* **BOTTOM LEFT** *Coy* **BOTTOM RIGHT** *In the Eye of the Beholder;* all from the *In the House of God* series

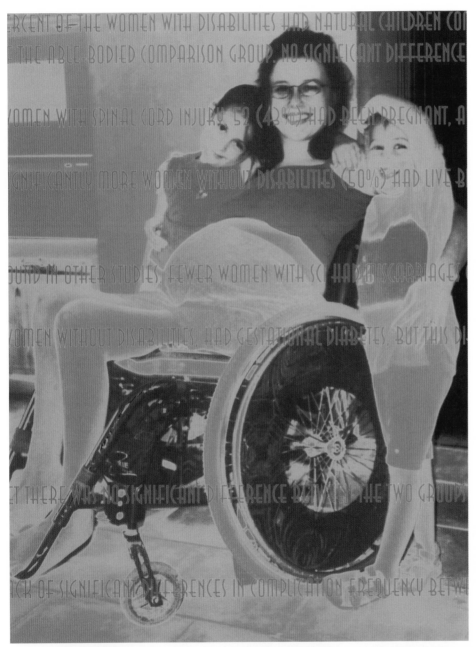

I am not looking to create a new and different world; I am seeking different responses to the one we have.

This work is based on a text I found on the Internet that highlighted the scientific "lack of significant difference" between disabled and nondisabled women in pregnancy and childbirth; it encouraged medical practitioners to "let" today's disabled women have children.

For me, motherhood brought with it new depths of independence, acceptance, and redemption from the alienation of a body in rebellion. Had my disability happened to my mother, (in the unlikely event that she could have survived it) her life would have been one of separation and institutions. Parenthood would have been unthinkable; routine sterilization of disabled women continued until relatively recently.

However, women with disabilities all over the world are starting to say, "I can" — and their children agree.

JESS LOSEBY • UNITED KINGDOM

Jess Loseby is a digital artist from England whose main medium is the Internet. Her work ranges from small and intimate online installations to large-scale digital projections and video. Her work crosses a variety of mediums and platforms, from mobile phones to large digital sculptures. Jess has three children, two wheels, one husband, and zero time.

ABOVE *Lack of Significant Difference*

FAKHRIYA AL-YAHYAI • OMAN

Fakhriya Al-Yahyai lives in the Sultanate of Oman, where her photographic work is influenced by Middle Eastern women's relationships to the colors of their fabrics — especially the color black, which is not a color of grieving, but the color of the everyday dress worn on top of finer clothes.

BELOW *Another Way of Seeing*

In the Middle East, we cover our everyday clothes with a long black gown. Beautiful fabrics hide underneath these black gowns. In my work, I want to let the viewer see the colors, shapes, themes, and patterns of these textiles from my culture. By letting the viewers see the hidden fabrics in as much detail as I see them myself, I seek to show the beauty of our clothes.

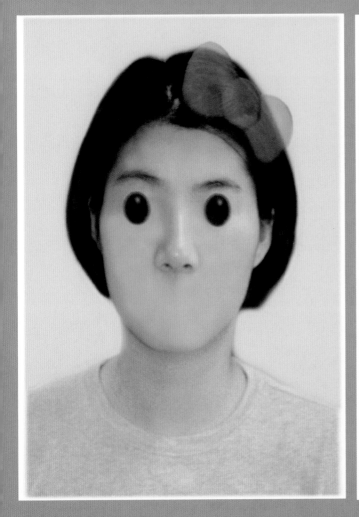
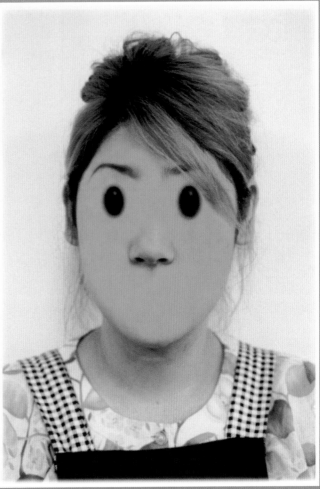

Hello Kitty is a popular character from Japan. She has long been loved by children in Asia, and her popularity is increasing in the United States and everywhere; her presence is spreading among many people.

On an unconscious level, Hello Kitty represents the ideals typically sought by women in Asia, but Kitty lives in London with her mama, papa, and twin sister. She maintains a lifestyle that appears to be Western. Her multicultural existence symbolizes generosity, innocence, kindness, and, most important, friendship.

Hello Kitty is also attached to the phrase "Kitty is curious." She is a contradiction. Her existence stands for curiosity, but she is not able to speak up. She is intentionally made voiceless, with no mouth. For that reason, she is welcomed as a safe symbol of curiosity.

INHEE JUNG · REPUBLIC OF KOREA

Inhee Jung was born in the small town of Cheun-Ahn in South Korea in 1972, and she was also educated there. She initially studied science but later changed direction to create new forms of visual language, focusing on themes related to silence and the experience thereof.

ABOVE *Being Kittyed 1* and *2*

FAMILY& RELATIONSHIPS

ZENA EL-KHALIL • LEBANON / UNITED KINGDOM

Zena el-Khalil was born in England in 1976 and grew up in Nigeria, where she read a lot, participated in karate competitions, and listened to Iron Maiden. Later, she moved to Lebanon and attended the American University of Beirut. She obtained her master of fine arts in 2002 from the School of Visual Arts in New York, but after realizing that everything she ever wanted in life was in Beirut, she moved back there. She presently lives in Beirut with her husband, Wael, a Greenpeace Rainbow Warrior, and her Jack Russell terrier, Tampopo. In 2003, as an exploration of the complexities of marriage in Lebanon, Zena did a performance piece during the First International Beirut Marathon. For the piece, she wore a wedding dress she had spray-painted shocking pink (as seen in the photograph on the facing page) and interviewed the runners about issues related to marriage.

LEFT *"Wahad Areese, Please!" (A Husband, Please!)*

SHEN LING · CHINA

Shen Ling's work focuses on narratives of the human condition, in ways that poke fun at people's capacity for self-satisfaction. She explores a wide range of emotional truths, often addressing sexuality and pleasure in contemporary Chinese life. She resides in the Chaoyang district of Beijing.

BELOW *Soaked in the Bath of Desire* series

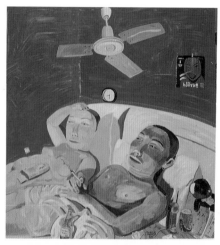

This series of paintings reflects the pursuit of a harmonious romantic life. The women in these pictures are eager to enjoy the pleasures of romantic relationships, but at the same time, they are inhibited by traditional morals about sexuality. When they finally break these chains, they begin to enjoy themselves and increase their own sense of satisfaction.

这个图片系列反映了对和谐、浪漫生活的追求。图片中的女人渴望享受罗曼蒂克式的幸福,可与此同时,她们又受到传统性道德的压制。当她们最终冲破了这些枷锁,她们才开始欣赏自己并增进了自我满足感

[FROM THE ORIGINAL CHINESE]

The women of my generation are living a moment of mutated concepts. They don't want unhappy marriages, but they still cry about not accomplishing Cinderella's dream of living happily ever after. They don't condemn themselves for having a forbidden love affair, but society still condemns them. They feel guilty for leaving their children to go to work, but they still want to teach them, by their own example, to struggle for what they wish for.

STELLA NANNI • BRAZIL

Stella Nanni, born in Brazil in 1972, began her artistic career by painting portraits. Emotion and intuition greatly influence her gestural, vibrant paintings, in which she portrays human feelings in everyday situations. Her sculptures and paintings have appeared in collections in Brazil, Chile, Argentina, Mexico, Portugal, Belgium, Italy, and Luxembourg.

ABOVE *Falling in Love*

A.CHUNG 2003

ANDREA CHUNG • USA

Andrea Chung was born in Newark, New Jersey, in 1978 and graduated from Parsons School of Design in New York City. She has exhibited her paintings across the United States and has had three solo exhibitions in Brooklyn, New York. She previously took part in the Okayplayer Tour, an eclectic montage of soul singers and organic rappers, where she sketched live drawings from the stage performances.

LEFT *Hope II*

Now

now
there is light coming in
through the crack in the door

now
there is hope
where i'd never expect it before

now
there are so many things
but there's nothing at all

now
you are learning to stand
i am learning to fall.

now
as the air in the night
becomes cooler and sweet

now
i get up seven times
just to cover his feet

now
there is pain
but i've packed it away for next year

now
there is newness and grace and for now,
there's no fear.

then
i can hardly remember what then used to be

then
there was someone i knew
looked exactly like me

i was running and running
with so much to boast

and i had no idea
what matters the most

later
when all of this has turned to songs
and faded pics

later
when colored wooden blocks
turn into heavy bricks

later
when you will greet me only
with the shyest smile

who knows what later brings?
and so meanwhile . . .

now
there is light coming in
through the crack in the door

now
there is hope
where i'd never expect it before

now
there are so many things
but there's nothing at all

now
you are learning to stand
i am learning to fall.

as i write these words, i am feeling tired, which is not new, as i have been feeling tired every day for two and a half years, since an enormous earthquake, tornado, thunderstorm, and atom bomb hit my life all at the same time. yes, my son was born and that was that. i spent thirty-one years before that day preparing for its arrival, for "the return of the king." of course, i had not the faintest clue that's what i was doing. so many years spent focusing, bettering, falling, kicking, striving, arriving, not arriving, hoping, dreaming, preening, screaming, laughing, flirting, hurting, crying, lying, creating, waiting, running, running, winning, spinning, growing, knowing, not knowing, sowing . . . and then, he appeared. like the first woman on earth to give birth. that was me. that's what i am.

    so now, there is light coming in through the crack in the door. no less, no more.

    now, i am still the same. and i will never be the same. . . .

    now, if the angel of death comes down and asks for his soul (the king's), he gets mine instead, no question about it.

    now, i am going to sleep.

    love, noa

NOA (ACHINOAM NINI) · ISRAEL

An Israeli musician with Yemeni roots, Noa is well known in Israel, in the United States, and globally. She has sung for Pope John Paul II, Bill Clinton, Steven Spielberg, and Yitzhak Rabin and has performed on stage with Sting, Stevie Wonder, Carlos Santana, Sheryl Crow, and many others. Her latest album, titled *Now,* was released internationally in 2002 by Universal Records.

LEFT Lyrics to "Now" from the album *Now*

A Wind Untamed

Every morning, she mixed with the crowds that stormed the arriving bus. It was hard to find a job in her profession in her little town, so she had to commute to the regional capital. The return commute was also tough; the winning strategy was to sneak onto the bus shielded by someone else's broad back. If for some reason that did not work, she could always stick out her hand holding the briefcase and let the crowd suck her into the bus's warm womb. The only tricky part was not letting go of the case.

Right now commuting seemed like a bad dream. She had a week's vacation ahead of her, and she didn't care that it was unpaid. The knocking of train wheels, usually grating, sounded to her like a hymn to a new life. She was traveling not to relax, not to shop, not to worship at cultural shrines. Her trip was an attempt to alter her fate. An attempt to stop retailing her brains for pocket change. An attempt to leave behind a city whose dark windy streets were filled with unhappy people who did not know how to smile, a place where one could plan no further than tomorrow, where life was full of uncertainty and fear. In that city her peers never dreamed of having children because they could not imagine how they would be able to provide for them. So they didn't want them. What did they want? Quick sex enjoyed strictly within the limits of easy friendship, free of any obligations.

Jeff H., a promising financial analyst from sunny Oklahoma, wanted to have kids. He wanted them to grow up bilingual. He assumed his Russian was fairly good because he had worked for three years in Saint Petersburg. In his first letter he wrote about his love for the city and his desire to marry a Russian woman.

"He looks like Chip and Dale rolled into one," she thought when examining his picture. Apart from this odd love for Russia, Jeff seemed to her a typical American, pragmatic and businesslike. This impression clashed with his stated hobby. "I love adventure," he wrote. "I love new people, new countries. I love discovering new things since I easily get bored."

"It seems that I am to become his new adventure. . . ." They agreed to meet at the entrance to the Nevsky Prospekt metro station.

The hands of the clock were steadily crawling towards five. The hurrying crowds flowed indifferently around a man who stood by the metro wearing a gray coat, which seemed too light for the Saint Petersburg winter. The man kept checking his watch. He left when the evening light drained down into the Neva River and the pink brush of sunset touched the green wintry sky. Several days later, he found her email in his in-box.

"Thank you for having come. When I was traveling to Saint Petersburg, I thought that only a few steps separated me from a happy future. Forgive me, but I did not dare approach you. I saw your eyes, and it seemed to me they were looking for someone extraordinary. There is nothing exceptional about me! The picture that I sent you looks better than I do in real life; it happens sometimes. In the picture, I look like a tender, shy Russian girl in whose eyes froze a dream of a tranquil life with a comfortable home, lovely children, and a solid husband who can take care of his family. I'm sure you are tired of the triumphant smiles of American ladies, who are too strong to need anybody. I could become your wife. But for that I would have to bury my true self. It seemed to me that you were seeking someone timid and dependent. I might have appeared timid and dependent in my letters to you, yet I am strong. I was afraid that I couldn't fulfill the Western idea of the patient, agreeable Russian woman. I was afraid

LADA KARITSKAYA • RUSSIA

Lada Karitskaya holds a bachelor of arts in philology and lives and works as a journalist in Severomorsk, a naval city in the Murmansk region of Russia. She was born in 1974.

that you wouldn't like me. I don't want to deceive you from the beginning. Yes, I am tired of this boring, gray life, and I want comfort, warmth, a family. But marriage without love is impossible for me. My ethics prohibit me from giving up my freedom in exchange for your sponsorship. When I saw you, you seemed so lonely, as if you had lost hope forever. Sweet sadness poisoned my joy then. It was like a dream that did not come true. It was like the wind that could not be tamed."

For the rest of the day, she wandered aimlessly up and down Nevsky Prospekt, trying not to think about the man in a gray coat waiting for her in vain at the entrance to the metro. The air rang with freedom and abandon.

"Some fashionable writer once said that Saint Petersburg can only be loved. There's nothing to do here but love, he said. So I'll love. I will love all its different guises: the wet and windy city of the winter, the dusty and humid city of the summer. At least this love will be reciprocated."

The white flames of a January day are put out by the black ink of the night. The late moon hangs in the pale sky like a round of moldy cheese. Its light pours through the window and fills the room. The silence, held captive by four walls, seems sinister and mysterious.

The woman sleeps. She dreams of a city washed by the spring rain, of asphalt turned blue with puddles, of constellations of streets awakened by the chittering birds. The sun's rays are dancing on the fierce green leaves and on the dazzling gold cupolas of Saint Isaac's. She smiles in her sleep.

"It's time to learn to live in the now. Time to trust that tomorrow will come without fail, and then everything will begin anew."

Женщина спит. Ей снится город, омытый весенним дождем, асфальт, ставший голубым от множества луж, созвездья улиц, разбуженных криками птиц. Солнечные лучи пляшут на пронзительной зелени листьев, на ослепительном золоте куполов Исаакия. И Она улыбается во сне. "Пора бы научиться жить сегодняшним днем. Свято верить, что непременно наступит завтра. И все начнется сначала."

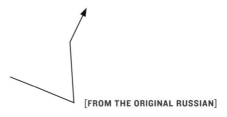

[FROM THE ORIGINAL RUSSIAN]

Old Maid

You keep asking me
why I still haven't married.
This time, I didn't find it funny.
I looked around to search for answers:
Perhaps they're written in my poems.
Perhaps they're sketched in my paintings.
Perhaps they're framed in my films.
I tried hard to remember
if this is what I chose:
the camera instead of the casserole,
the canvas instead of the cradle,
the metaphor instead of a mate.

You're still asking me
why I still don't have a companion.
Never did I consider
being single
a curse.
I won't look around for a while
even if you ask one more time.
The answer might still be long in coming.

Soltera

Tinatanong mo pa rin hanggang ngayon
kung bakit hindi pa ako nag-aasawa.
Sa pagkakataong ito, hindi na ako natawa.
Luminga akong naghanap ng mga sagot:
Baka nakalista sa aking mga tula.
Baka nakaguhit sa aking mga pintura.
Baka nakaeksena sa aking mga pelikula.
Pinilit kong tandaan
kung ito ba ang pinagpilian:
ang kamera kaysa sa kaserola,
ang kanbas kaysa sa kuna,
ang talinghaga kaysa sa asawa.

Tinatanong mo pa rin hanggang ngayon
kung bakit wala pa rin akong kasama.
Kahit kelan hindi ko inisip
na ang pag-iisa
ay isang sumpa.
Hindi na muna ako lilinga,
magtanong ka man isang beses pa.
Baka ang darating na sagot ay matagal pa.

[FROM THE ORIGINAL TAGALOG]

VIVIAN N. LIMPIN • PHILIPPINES

Vivian N. Limpin, born in Manila, graduated with a degree in creative writing from the University of the Philippines. She also works with the visual and performing arts and participates with various nonprofits and a women's network called KASI-BULAN, all dedicated to increasing women's participation in the arts sector.

JOLIVETTE MECENAS • USA

After working as a photo editor, a PR lackey for Big Oil, and a pixel pusher during that historical capitalist romp known as the dot-com boom, Jolivette Mecenas has accepted — happily — a life of teaching and writing. She is teaching at the University of Hawaii while pursuing her PhD in English, after which she plans to return to her native land, California.

One Is Not the Loneliest Number

"One cannot think well, love well, sleep well, if one has not dined well."
Virginia Woolf

There are several life skills my mother taught me before I set off into the world: how to properly separate my laundry; how to balance my checkbook; how to prepare red meat in an assortment of quick-and-easy ways. Other skills I picked up as a sink-or-swim necessity: how to negotiate rent; how to negotiate salary increases; how to negotiate failed relationships, hopeless heartache, the metaphysical realization that we die; and how to negotiate reasonable rates with the psychotherapist. There are certain skills, however, that are often left out of public discourse, usually owing to our general squeamishness about anxiety-arousing issues such as mental illness, poverty, sexual dysfunction, and — what I would like to expound upon in this essay — being single. Or more specifically, being a single diner.

To walk into a restaurant by yourself on a Friday night, request a table for one, savor a full-course meal complete with wine, and linger over your espresso while surrounded by tables of raucous friends or (even worse) affectionate lovers spooning gelato into each other's mouths — to dine alone in supreme grace and dignity is a life skill akin to high art. Your mother never taught you this. Probably because she never spelled it out for you that at certain points of your life, *you will be alone.* If you are not now or have not already been alone, you will be

one day. And if you already are, welcome. The purpose of this essay is to reclaim the state of dining alone and to overthrow cultural assumptions that cow us into spending another desolate evening eating microwaved burritos while watching *The Jeffersons* on TV.

I admit, there are few things I enjoy more than sharing a meal with friends, either at home or at a restaurant; the conversation and laughter flow, we reminisce about old times, the palates are soothed and happy. Dining with a lover is usually a notch higher on the Richter scale of pleasant evenings, adding the element of being pampered and serviced by the wait staff, leaving us to concentrate on *l'affaire d'amour* in between bites of mu shu pork. But there are times in my life when I find myself far away from friends and even further away from having a lover. At these moments, I stubbornly refuse to give up the one epicurean pleasure I can truly satisfy by myself: eating. Why *not* go to a restaurant by myself? I don't remember the first time I did, but I have many times since, and my experiences lead me to believe that the lone diner strikes an assortment of anxious emotions within people's hearts. Whether it is fear ("Will I be her one day?") or pity ("That poor girl!") or relief ("Thank God I'm engaged to Bobby!"), most people would rather the single young woman dine alone in the privacy of her home, and not in public. However, I refuse to compromise my life to soothe the anxieties of others. In order to subvert the subtle discrimination against solo diners, we must first learn to identify it.

To begin, there are certain recurring reactions that happen whenever I dine alone, designed, I'm sure, to discourage the act. Most of these reactions fall under what I term *single-phobia,* or

continued

the irrational fear of independent people engaging in social activities by themselves. A dining experience in which I am harassed by single-phobia usually unfolds in the following manner:

Host: Table for . . . ?

Me: One, please.

Host: (Arching a skeptical eyebrow) Okaaay . . . this way, please.

(The host then leads me past bright empty booths at the front of the restaurant to a shaky miniscule table in a dark corner next to the kitchen.)

Me: Couldn't I have one of those front tables? I'd rather not sit in the dark.

Host: I'm sorry, but those tables are reserved for parties of two or more. (What he really means to say is that the front tables are reserved for people with friends and social lives, and that people dine at restaurants to have a good time in the company of others. To maintain the festive atmosphere, they relegate me to the dark corner.)

Me: Fine.

(I am seated. The waiter takes my order nearly twenty minutes later. He only returns twice more, to bring food and to bring my check. He easily ignores my frantic hand gestures for more water, my polite yet assertive yelps of "Excuse me!" and focuses on any other place in the room when hustling past my table in and out of the kitchen. I know what he's thinking, having been in the restaurant business myself: single diner equals small tip.)

Why does single-phobia permeate our culture? Perhaps we can blame the usual suspects: magazines, MTV, Top 40 boy-bands crooning their everlasting love to pubescent girls, urban bar culture (straight and gay), romantic comedies with trite endings, advertisements with ludicrous claims. But whatever the reasons, the object of the game is to not be alone. People spend lots of cash to be in a couple. Couples spend lots of cash being in couples. Call it a capitalist theory of modern love or just call me bitter, but whatever the explanation, this cultural phenomenon of anti-aloneness prevails wherever I attempt to enjoy a meal in a restaurant by myself.

For example, once when I was in New York City, I spent one homeless week in the Lucky Wagon, a pit passing for a hotel on the Chinatown–Little Italy border. At that point, I had only a hulking backpack of possessions, a pseudoglamorous magazine job paying subsistence wages, and a crazed determinism to keep me from ending up in the East River. My five-by-ten whitewashed room had no TV set to quell the voices in my head demanding of me, "How did you end up at this all-time low?" I tried to soothe my worries with dinner on Mulberry Street, the vivacious tourist trap of Italian eateries, where I chose a noisy, crowded little trattoria because it served my favorite dish, *penne all'arrabiata* — "angry pasta" for an angry girl.

The waiter sat me at a corner table, of course, me being the only single diner in a room full of birthday parties and groups of Japanese tourists. He was a handsome, young Italian American, his name may have been Anthony, and he laughed and joked with me for a bit. Then, broadcasting over the entire room in a booming voice, he asked me, "What are you doing eating alone?" Flushed from embarrassment and the wine, I shrugged my shoulders. "It's Saturday night and you're alone? What's the matter, your boyfriend doesn't take you out???" I started to explain that I didn't have a boyfriend to take me out, that I didn't even have any friends in New York, that I really was *alone*, but I realized he wouldn't believe me. That's when I began to understand how deeply entrenched in American culture the fear of the single diner is. It didn't even cross Anthony's mind that I was an independent, free being, eating dinner by myself.

Don't be mistaken, I'm not some kind of gourmand misanthrope advocating antisocial behavior. I recognize the basic human need to feel love and affection. But I also believe that a young woman would do well for herself to recognize her relationship to the world and the conditions in the world that cause her to experience what our modernist friends the Existentialists called *angst,* or the feeling of despair and anguish. Night after night of frozen burritos and TV sitcom reruns is this city-dwelling gal's version of despair and anguish. But then an epiphany: the realization that in any life of substance during which risks and leaps of faith are taken, there are inevitably moments when there is only me, and that is a good thing, and I will celebrate by taking myself out as my favorite guest to a lovely dinner.

With all self-affirmations out of the way, I'd like to proceed with tips and techniques for interested parties on how to dine alone gracefully and enjoyably.

- First of all, the meal you are eating determines whether or not you may bring reading material to entertain yourself. I'm of the opinion that any brunch or lunch is a good time to bring the paper, a good book, a magazine, et cetera. If you forget to bring something, under no circumstances should you begin to shuffle through your Day Runner organizer, pretending to write notes in the mini-calendar section; it is a telltale sign that you are extremely uncomfortable dining alone and are desperate to look busy. Instead, calmly finish your meal and occupy yourself by staring blankly at people and eavesdropping blatantly on conversations. It's entertaining, and you'll seem intriguing, I guarantee.
- If you are eating at a more stylish restaurant, you might consider more sophisticated modes of self-entertainment, like drinking copiously. In restaurants with outdoor seating, I like to smoke. Be careful, though, not to drink or smoke too much before your meal is served, as you may make yourself ill, and that can get messy.

- One game I like to play every now and then when I'm dining at a finer eating establishment is "Food Critic": Dress to the nines for your meal. At several key points during the meal (after swirling the first taste of wine around in your glass and after the first bite of each dish), pull out a notebook and pen and jot down notes. Make several calls on your cell phone to your answering machine at home, pretending you are making after-dinner plans, and drop the names of chic bars and media personalities whenever possible. If I do a good job, I can usually weasel a free dessert and free alcohol. It's fun!

Before I conclude, I'd like to point out one very important thing to remember at all times: you are not really alone. Sure, the setting is for one and there is only a fake floral arrangement in a vase to greet you across the table. But who says you can't converse with the floral arrangement? People talk to their plants and pets all the time — why is it so strange to speak with inanimate objects? A short conversation I had with my dinner last night went something like this:

Me: Hello, Mr. Pizza! I must eat you now!

A rather flat conversation, I admit, but thoroughly spontaneous and enjoyable nonetheless. Or if you like, solo dinners are good opportunities to resurrect imaginary childhood friends and catch up on old times with them. During my solo meals, I like to replay past arguments I've lost to friends or ex-lovers, perfecting the flawless retort I wish I had thought of at the time. However, I have to be careful not to argue out loud, as I tend to get carried away and alarm people at nearby tables. My point is, when dining alone, never underestimate the pleasure of your own company, and enjoy it with pride. And when all else fails, there are always the voices in your head. . . .

A White Knight's Story

I remember fairy tales from my childhood days — all those stories about beautiful princesses and brave knights. I think all girls love those kinds of stories, and all girls dream about knights on white horses. We learn about love from fairy tales, and then we dream about this feeling; we wait for true love to come.

The world has changed. People have changed. It is fashionable now to change your social role: women and men don't want to limit their social functions. We are trying to blur the line between woman and man, but we don't think about what can happen when we finally achieve that.

My story is about a girl. She has been waiting for her knight for such a long time, so she decided to become a white knight herself. She thinks that it is probably possible to find a knight inside her if it is not possible to meet him somewhere around her.

 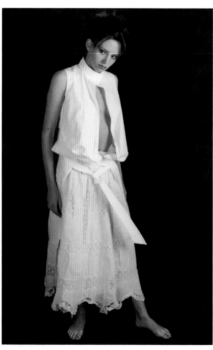 

ANNA ALEXANDROVA • RUSSIA

Anna Alexandrova lives in Saint Petersburg. She studied psychology at Saint Petersburg State University. In her spare time, she experiments with fashion design and volunteers at a rape crisis center. Her favorite book is *What's Holding You Back?* by Linda Austin.

ABOVE *A White Knight's Story* series

ROVENA AGOLLI • ALBANIA

Rovena Agolli is an Albanian artist living in Monterey, California.

BELOW *In All My Dreams*

Violence, especially towards women, is still a problem in many families in southeastern Europe, and particularly in my own country, Albania. The inability of women to erase the system of violence, and their silent acceptance of a horrible compromise, create the facade of a happy family.

SELF-DEVELOPMENT

CHRISTINE POLOWYJ • AUSTRALIA

Of direct Ukrainian lineage, Christine Polowyj was born in England in 1975 and moved to Australia in 1983. Her grandparents' tragic experiences during and after World War II and her mother's untimely death profoundly influenced her life and work. In her artwork, she strives to inspire others to confront and express positively their own difficult histories and emotions.

LEFT *Self-Portrait*

My mother once told me after reading my work, "I don't know if you're brave or shameless." Maybe I am a little bit of both. The women of my generation are in the position of stepping forth and claiming their space. Given the privileges gained by our mothers' and grandmothers' struggles, we now have a little ground to stand on. And not only are we using it, but we are continually pushing the boundaries back with our actions and our voices.

So thank you, Alice Walker, Toni Morrison, Sonia Sanchez, Theresa Hak Kyung Cha, Jessica Hagedorn, Ntozake Shange, Sandra Cisneros, Arundhati Roy — for being proud, unforgiving, passionate women, in life and on the page. I hope we can look at ourselves honestly and leave a record of our lives as beautifully as you have. So we can all add to the dialogue of what it means to be human, and woman, in this world.

ISHLE YI PARK · USA

Ishle Yi Park was born in 1977 to Korean immigrant parents who have run a fish store her whole life. She is currently the Poet Laureate of Queens, New York, and a cast member of the Tony Award–winning *Def Poetry Jam* tour, but on Christmas she still goes back home to help her parents at the fish store. Her first book of poetry, *The Temperature of This Water*, was published in 2004 by Kaya Press.

Autobiography at 25

I am 25 years old,
and I tell stories and lies —

I've lost my youth and two men I've loved,
I've lost most of my mother tongue,
I've lost or given up seven babies,

I've memorized songs of Bob Marley, 10 of my own poems
and one from Sue Kwok Kim who wrote,
Did you ever see a stone so lonely
it leapt into the sea?

I've memorized the calm in my lover's face when
he holds me in sleep,
I've made love to eight men and two women,
each one a window: 5 open, 4 cracked, 1 broken,

I've prayed in churches, temples, an open field,
and the heart of my bed.

In 1996 my boyfriend and brother were arrested —
I spent my time shuffling between
Queens and Brooklyn courthouses,
giving my whole paycheck
to a lawyer who asked me to give him a massage on the 6 train.

In 1991 my parents split and my mother, brother, and I
moved into a one bedroom apartment in the projects
called Dara Gardens; we slept on the carpet & our kitchen
window opened to a brick wall. I learned to seek beauty alone,
on the rooftop behind McDonald's parking lot,
staring out into a sea of yellow reeds, in dry heat.

My mother, a hard woman,
did not weep often; she smoked mad Kents and sat alone.
I was 14, reading Malcolm X tucked in my book bag like a bible,
Alice Walker, Richard Wright, Toni Morrison. I wanted to believe
in freedom.

When I was 12, my best friend
and her brother were stabbed in their Long Island apartment.
And that was the year I first fell to the ground with grief,
in an empty parking lot where no one could hear me.

That was the first time someone I loved was taken from me.
That was the first time I wrote a real poem.

When I was nine my aunt bought me a red, cloth-covered diary.
When I was 4, I had my first crush on a girl in nursery school
and learned to keep that a secret.

When I was 2, in 1979, my parents owned a dirty white punchbuggy,
my father opened a fish store, and my mother bought milk
with food stamps. We lived in Astoria, Queens, and uma
dropped me off with the Puerto Ricans at the corner store bodega
because she couldn't afford a babysitter.

When I was 2, I saw my father
try to smother my mother with a pillow.

I tried to get in between. I still thought I could save her,
that was when I began the failed business of trying to save other people.
I am still learning to retire and invest in saving myself first.

When I was two the world was split into good and evil.
When I was two I stood in front of my parents' friends and told stories,
    and lies —

So listen. I will tell you where the story ends, or where it begins —

On May 24, 1977, my mother
rode the N train from Astoria to Manhattan, 9 months
pregnant and ready to birth me into the city.
Earlier that year, my parents loved each other
enough to pour stories into each other all night,
and my father named me issil, because maybe he thought
we could start new, like the fresh dew of the morning.

We are the generation who grew up watching television, drinking milk, and eating butter cakes. We are used to accepting more new things and playing more roles by ourselves. We are beautiful, sensitive, and apt to change. We change ourselves in order to better ourselves. We haven't experienced huge social transformations, but we've seen wars around us. We are used to thinking about the answers to this era, with whatever information available, but we don't have a specific political belief. We are a drifting generation. We experience the happiness that life brings us as well as the bitterness while we go through our living process. In this era, we suffer while we enjoy.

My works of art are a kind of record — nostalgia of past things and a reflection on the human situation. I have not forced myself to reflect as a female on purpose; however, the works themselves unintentionally reveal a female's instinct and concern, which makes my work somewhat different from a male artist's. In my grandmother's and mother's generations, women were regarded as appendages of men. This inequality in social status led to the budding of female consciousness. Women gradually came out of the family to face society and took on some social responsibilities. Today's society is a society of information. We have more opportunities and means to express ourselves than our mothers and grandmothers did. The challenge before me is how to continue to develop creative works derived from and inspired by life, because my feelings towards life cannot be fully expressed by a few works. Life continues, and so must my works.

[FROM THE ORIGINAL CHINESE]

我们是看着电视,喝着牛奶,吃着奶油蛋糕成长的一代,我们习惯接受更多的新奇事物 ,并在自己身上演义更多的角色。我们美丽,敏感又善变,我们改变自己希望做得更 好。我们没有经历巨大的社会变革,却目睹战争就发生在我们身边。我们习惯在一切可 能获得信息的领域里思考对这个时代的答案,但是又没有明确的政治信仰,我们是"飘 "一代。我们感受生活带给我们的快乐,在经历这种过程里也感受它带来的痛苦,我们 痛并快乐着,在这个时代。

自己的作品只是一种记录,对流逝物的迷恋和对人本身所处位置的思考,几乎没有刻意 去强求做一个"女性"的思考,作品里自然流露的女性动机和关注点,使自己在做作品 时和男性艺术家有了一定的差距。在祖母和母亲的年代,女性更多的作为男性的附庸, 社会地位的不平等导致那时女性意识的萌芽,女性逐渐从家庭走出来面对社会,也逐渐 承担起部分的社会责任。现今社会是信息的社会,我们得到更多的表达机会和表达途 径。自己所面临的挑战就是如何从生活中继续发展创作,因为对生命的感受不是几个作 品就能完成的,生命在继续,作品在继续

CHEN QIULIN • CHINA

Chen Qiulin was born in Hubei province, China, in 1975. She graduated from Sichuan Arts Institute in 2000. She now lives in Chengdu, China, and is a prominent performance artist. Her works of art show an ambiguous attitude towards Chinese traditional culture and reveal women's worries about their survival in modern times.

RIGHT *Self-Portrait* series

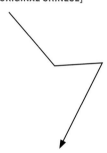

The basket on my shoulder is symbolic in this painting. In Uganda, baskets are seen most during the harvest seasons. Personally I feel I have arrived at a time of harvesting.

AMANDA TUMUSIIME • UGANDA

Amanda Tumusiime was born in Kaharo Kabale, Uganda, in 1973. She received a formal education in art from Makerere University in Uganda, where she continues to work as a lecturer for the School of Industrial and Fine Arts.

LEFT *Songs of Empowerment 2*

"T" Is for Triumph

[An Excerpt from *Amor, curiosidad, prozac, y dudas (Love, Curiosity, Prozac, and Doubts)*, translated by Michael J. Crooks]

You could say that every birthday is another brush stroke to add to what will become your definitive portrait. You could also say that each new year is a shovelful of dirt on the tomb of your youth. Each new year brings with it more experience, and therefore, so they say, more wisdom and serenity. Each birthday brings with it the punctual reminder of your conscience: this year you still haven't done anything with your life.

I turned thirty last month. I have squandered exactly one third of my existence.

"If you want to be successful as a businesswoman, you must stand up as often as your male colleagues and in the same situations they do. Do not stay seated when someone comes into your office or speaks with you in front of your desk. It does not matter what the rules of etiquette say: if you want equal opportunities and equal treatment, you must stand up like a man, literally and figuratively speaking."

Especially if you are as tall as or taller than most of your male colleagues.

"Behave like a man. Control your emotions. Do not cry in public. Ensure that your gestures are always suitable and appropriate to the situation at hand. Let your actions match your words."

"Prepare yourself for the worst. Remember that, in general, women who find themselves at the helm are the targets of criticisms that have nothing to do with their professional abilities. In addition, some of those qualities that are looked upon with respect and even admiration in an entrepreneurial man are transformed into negative qualities when assumed by a woman. If a woman concentrates all of her energy on work, she is called frustrated; if she surrounds herself with a team and shares responsibility, then she is labeled insecure; if she manages with a firm hand, they say she is embittered."

Thirty years old. A hundred thousand dollars a year. A BMW. My own apartment. No prospects of marriage or children. No one who cares for me in a special way. Is that so depressing? I don't know. Is it that little green and white pill that I take every morning that stops me from crying? Is it that little pill that the doctor prescribed me, that miraculous concentration of fluoxetine, that makes my worries slide over me like drops of water across a greasy frying pan?

Is this peace or Prozac? I don't know.

Thirty years old. The beginnings of maturity. A meaningful date that had to be celebrated.

But I didn't want to organize a birthday party because in truth I didn't have anyone to invite. My sisters and my mother, of course, but do I really love them? Yes, to a certain point. They are my family. They always have been and always will be.

My mother and my sisters are the only fixed reference point in my life. For me, my mother will always be the Enigma from Another Planet, so icy and distant, so restrained, but she has treated me well, and above all, she has always been there, unmovable like a milestone marking a trailhead.

My sister Ana is a saint, a good girl in every sense of the word, but terribly boring just like all good girls, and not exactly the kind of person you want to see on your birthday.

And Cristina . . . okay, it has to be said. Yes, I had hated her with all my heart, but maybe that was just because I loved her so much. Still, I didn't feel like celebrating my birthday with an intimate dinner with Cristina. We didn't get along well enough for that.

I could also organize a big party and invite work colleagues and their wives, old acquaintances from college, clients, and suppliers.

"When you set out to organize a get-together, you should always keep four fundamental points in

LUCÍA ETXEBARRÍA • SPAIN

Lucía Etxebarría was born in the Basque country in 1966, though most of her life has unfolded in Madrid and Valencia. She is a diverse and accomplished writer who has published poetry, novels, and essays and has worked on several film scripts. Her work has been translated into more than eight languages. Lucía is also a journalist and has written for well-known magazines and newspapers such as the Spanish daily *El Mundo*.

mind: What kind of party do I want? Who should I invite? When should I plan it for? And Where should I hold it?"

"Only invite those people who should be there. Only invite those who you are prepared to listen to. Do not stand by protocol when selecting the guests. Leave enough time for preparations. Set a date for when all the most important guests are available. Do not forget to be courteous. Calculate costs. Check out the state of the place."

"If you approach the party knowing exactly what you want, it is quite possible that you will leave it having achieved just that."

This was even less appealing.

Hours of preparation and who knows how much money spent on hors d'oeuvres and drinks so that a load of people can invade the privacy of my home, cutting up the air with their meaningless chatter and faked laughter. And the next day all that is left is a major hangover, cigarette ash and sticky lumps on the Formica table and floor, bottles spilled all over the kitchen, overturned plastic cups everywhere, and dirty napkins and plates forgotten on top of bookshelves.

No, thank you. No parties for me.

I decided to ask for the day off, hopped in my BMW, and headed south. Twelve hours at the wheel, listening to Schubert's Lieder on maximum volume. I didn't stop until I reached Fuengirola. It must have been around six o'clock in the evening.

Twenty-two years had passed.

Twenty-two years since that summer in Fuengirola. The last summer that we spent with my father.

The town had changed a lot. Huge white buildings along the beachfront, enormous brick obscenities, cement and glass giants looking straight out to sea, perfectly square like bunkers. And at their feet, like ants, slews of beach bars and snack places now closed, announcing their calamari and salads in strident posters made of cheap plastic, advertisements in loud colors overrun with spelling mistakes.

It was an off-season Wednesday and the beach was deserted.

I sat down on the terrace of the only open bar I could find and ordered one glass of wine after another. I was resolved to drink thirty glasses, one for each of my thirty years, but I can't remember how many I drank. At a certain point I must have lost track.

And I drank glass after glass, slowly, while looking at that vast cream-colored expanse that was the beach. The hours passed by and the landscape changed color.

The sky kept transforming, alternatively light blue, indigo, cobalt, deep blue, violet. The sea went from bottle green to emerald to dark green. The sand acquired all of the warm colors on the spectrum, ochre, amber, chestnut, brown, rust. In my drunkenness the landscape turned into a kaleidoscope, a chromatic delirium.

Night finally fell and all the colors melted into black.

So I headed towards the beach to count the stars.

One or two hours must have passed. I was extremely cold, and on top of that, I was thirty. Not a soul was on the beach. Just me, the sand, the water, and the stars.

I stood up and stayed there staring at the black water, practically flat and unmoving except for a few tiny waves, subtle horizontal white lines of foam, sliding slowly towards the beach.

I began to think that I could walk into the water, walk and walk until I could no longer touch the bottom, and drown just like that. Like Virginia Woolf.

continued

To die young and with elegance.

If you can resist the natural urge to swim to the surface to take a breath, then asphyxiation in water is the least painful way to die. It's even pleasant. A very sweet death. The lack of oxygen causes you to hallucinate, and without knowing what is happening, you drift away in a kind of ecstasy[. . . .]

The sea would be my final lover. The waves would give me the kiss of death[. . . .]

I would arrive in a sub-marine country where there was no space for fear, ugly thoughts, disloyalties, rancor, unfortunate love, bitterness, melancholy, nostalgia, and wanting to cry. I would look happily upon this blank slate of peace that death had furnished.

But even as I entered the water, I knew that I would not have the courage to drown myself. I was feeling an intense desire to finish everything, but I did not have the strength of will necessary to do it. I had no reason to continue living, but I was not suffering with sufficient intensity to be capable of cutting off my own breath.

Ahead of me were years of men who I would not understand, and a world of confusion I would have to struggle with daily; a world where families disintegrate and human relationships make no sense. A world where there was only room for triumph. And to achieve this you have to sacrifice almost everything else.

When fate calls you to this place . . .

I was not afraid. Death did not scare me.

It did not cross my mind that in reality, the only thing that scared me was to go on living.

The next thing I remember is waking up numb, with my mouth as dry as cork and an intermittent pounding in my temples. The sun was already fairly high in the sky, and the warm sand was like a comforting nest. I had fallen asleep, my conscience dulled by the wine, lulled by the hypnotic murmur of the waves.

"When faced with a crisis situation, make a list of available alternatives and divide them into categories of desirable and undesirable. Consider the matter as if it were already decided and evaluate your decision. Repeat this process with all possible outcomes that you can imagine. Mentally eliminate any hurdles. Invent analogies. Break the mold of logical thought when analyzing the crisis situation. And most importantly, always have at hand a Plan B to be used in case of emergencies. Your Plan B will give you a sense of security that will allow you to take risks and do what is needed to triumph."

Therein lay my error. I had not thought of a Plan B. I had laid all my cards on the table in one single hand, and now that this had not worked, now that I realized that my winnings scarcely covered my losses, I did not know how to go on. What should you do when you discover that you have lived your life according to the desires of others, convinced that you were pursuing your own ambitions?

And as I drove back to Madrid, faced with the prospect of confronting an infinite succession of identical days, gray, blurry and dull, alone, enslaved, condemned to playing the pawn in a game I did not understand, without companions or lovers, without children, without close friends, I thought more than once about letting go of the steering wheel and allowing the car to lose control around a curve.

But I didn't, because deep down I am exactly like my computer, with its emergency battery ready to connect automatically in case of electrical failure.

Designed to last. Programmed to keep going.

The Past Decade

I graduated as a teacher but secretly wanted to be a journalist or a dancer. I have been an English teacher everywhere from London to a remote university in northwest China. I have been to twenty countries. I have been a waitress (many times in Melbourne, and at the Edinburgh airport), a nude artist's model, an art gallery curator, an exhibition curator in Chinese villages, a TV news editor, a photographer, a performer, an activist. >> >>

MARCELA NIEVAS · AUSTRALIA / ARGENTINA

Marcela Nievas is a photographer, performer, teacher, community arts practitioner, traveler, and dreamer. She has a master's degree in social sciences, international development, and anthropology. In much of her artwork, she focuses on the experiences of women.

continued

I have sung in Chinese on the back of a live buffalo for a national TV show in China and a live audience of thirty thousand, and I have danced on a boathouse in Prague — and got paid for both! I have assisted my mother and sister in childbirth. I have been in love and have been loved many times. I have destroyed love and felt the darkness of loneliness. I have been lost in depression. I have climbed Mount Olympus in Greece. I have lived in a former brothel in London and with ten musicians in a factory in Melbourne. I have made many friends scattered across the planet. I have published a short story. I have had a solo photography exhibition. Several newspaper articles have been written about me. After ten years, I have returned to university. I have been chosen to work as a visual artist in Spain next year. I have started to learn how to forgive myself for mistakes. . . .

I look forward to falling in love, really in love, looking into the eyes of my children, laughing a lot, gaining more knowledge and maybe even a little wisdom, continuing to create as a photographer and performer, being inspired by people and places, working towards a better world, discovering new paths.

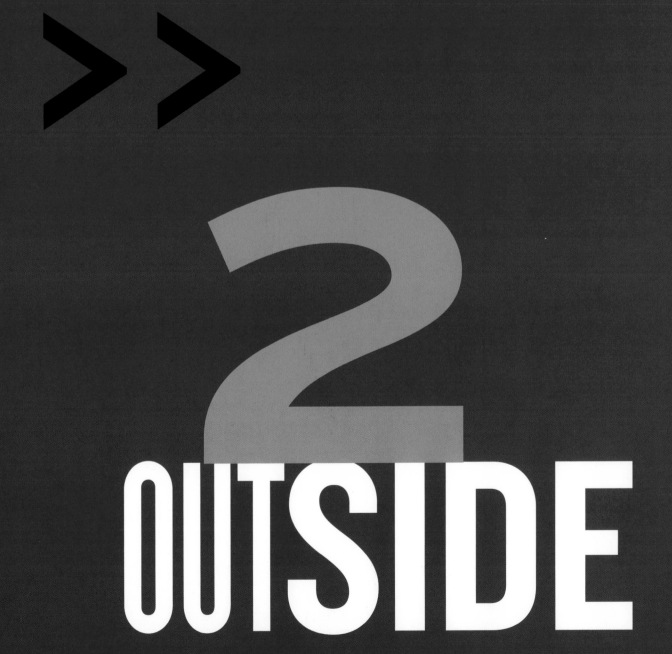

>>

2

OUTSIDE

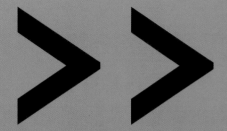

IT MAY RANK

as one of the largest and most rapid demographic shifts in world history: from the 1970s until today, millions of women across the world have attended primary and secondary schools in countries where their mothers and grandmothers never had such opportunities.

And that's not all. We've also entered the workforce in huge numbers. While many inequalities in pay and access still exist, the experience of being a professional working mother is one that increasingly draws together women from dramatically different geographic and economic backgrounds — from Nasra Abubakar in Somalia, the daughter of a camel farmer who is the first in her family to go to college, to Karenna Gore Schiff, the daughter of a former U.S. vice president.

The entries in this part are snapshots of young women engaged with the larger world, the world outside of their homes and outside of the intimacies of their personal lives. They are portraits of young women in the public sphere in an age when access to and mobility within that sphere are increasing for many women.

We begin with a short section on the important roles that communities play in our public lives. Dilrabo Inomova tells us how a group of women in a small town in Tajikistan came together to rebuild their community after it was devastated by civil war; her piece illustrates the importance of women uniting as a group to overcome adversity. Indeed, women have played a key role in fostering reconciliation after some of the most violent conflicts of our era, such as those in Bosnia and Rwanda. Another theme that emerges in this section is the idea of *digital* community. Yee-Ming Tan from Malaysia (now living in Hong Kong) talks about using email, phone, and text messaging to maintain a support network among friends and family who live on other continents. Remarking on her relationship with her family, who are scattered across Asia and Europe, Yee-Ming writes, "We are connected emotionally and spiritually but not physically anymore."

The next section of part 2, on work, gives a taste of the diversity of sectors in which women are employed. The dramatic entry of young women into the professional workforce is exemplified by the work of women like Hala El Koussy, whose photo essay shows a young woman who goes off every day to a well-paid position in a large construction company in Cairo while her maid tends to her house. However, informal employment remains an important source of revenue for women in much of the world. Siti Norkhalbi Haji Wahsalfelah shares beautiful photographs of women's involvement in the traditional textile industry in Brunei Darussalam. Omotoyosi Odunsi's portraits of "baby women" in Lagos, Nigeria, remind us of the many young women living in poverty who are forced into prostitution to make a living.

The last section of this part is a series on power — and these entries do not present a candy-coated view of things. There is the issue of AIDS, which disproportionately affects young women in Africa, and about which HIV-positive activist Prudence Nobantu Mabele speaks eloquently. There is the question of women's status under religious law, an issue that Hafsat Abiola from Nigeria addresses with great sensitivity and courage. There is the question of the explosive tensions between the United States and the larger Muslim world — a concern shared by American journalist Lisa Ling and Jordanian Queen Rania Al-Abdullah, both of whom comment on the need for greater understanding across societies.

What unites all of these pieces is the fact that their authors are actively engaged in the effort to transform the social issues that they write about. In fact, what may be a signature of our generation is not merely the number of young women who are educated, employed, and actively working to resolve the problems that they face, but also the positive, can-do attitude with which they are doing it.

Take Marama Davidson, a young professional who is working in New Zealand on behalf of the indigenous Mäori people. She tells us in plain terms that her people still face severe discrimination and poverty; things haven't necessarily improved over the past thirty years. But she concludes her essay by stating that she does not let these problems define her — she only lets them guide her to the work that needs to be done. She chooses to center herself in the things she loves most: her family and her people's precious cultural heritage.

Marama's example says it best: we are a generation of women who face problems but don't define ourselves by them.

FACTS & TRENDS

>> Women's enrollment in higher education has increased markedly in most regions of the world. In the Caribbean and western Asia, for example, it has surpassed that of men, and in South America, it is equal to that of men. Enrollment rates are higher for women than for men in many countries of Europe and in the United States and New Zealand.[1]

>> In southern Asia in 1980, just 35 percent of girls were in primary or secondary school, but by 1994 the number had increased to 64 percent. Over that same period in the Caribbean, the number rose from 83 to 93 percent.[2]

>> Since the 1970s literacy rates for women worldwide have risen from 54 percent to 64 percent. Studies conducted by the United Nations consistently show that all countries that have successfully reduced their population growth rate have one factor in common: a high female literacy rate.[3]

>> In 2003 1.1 billion (or 40 percent) of the world's 2.8 billion workers were women; this represents an increase of nearly 200 million women in formal employment between 1993 and 2003.[4]

>> Women spend twice as much or more time as men doing unpaid work. Worldwide, on average, women earn two-thirds of what men earn.[5]

>> As of 2005, sixty-eight women have served as heads of state worldwide. More than three-quarters of them took office since 1990.[6]

COMMUNITY

MARCELA NIEVAS • **AUSTRALIA / ARGENTINA**
For Marcela's bio and photo, please see page 81.

LEFT From the *Asian Women* series

MARIANNA MLYNÁRČIKOVÁ • SLOVAKIA

Photographer Marianna Mlynárčiková was born and raised in Banská Bystrica, Slovakia, where she currently tutors in the department of fine art at Matej Bel University. Her work documenting the lives of women in *Romani* (gypsy) communities throughout her country has been instrumental in efforts by local and international nonprofit organizations to better the conditions in these communities.

ABOVE AND RIGHT *Life of Roma Women from Šobov, Slovakia*

MARIKO KADIDIATOU • NIGER

Mariko Kadidiatou was born in 1976 in Tessaoua, Niger, where she still lives and works as an artist.

ABOVE *Femme Baobab: Mère d'Afrique (The Baobab Tree Woman: Mother of Africa)*

A woman is a baobab, the tree that builds the village. She is the head of the household. She has the responsibility for the whole family and for work. She rises with the sun and doesn't sleep before the sun sets.

In 2001 I journeyed to Mount Kailash in Tibet simply to fulfill a thirst for adventure, but the two-week trip provided a high dose of spiritual nourishment. The Tibetan women I met along the way embody what I see as the essence of womanhood — courage, endurance, strength, beauty, and joyfulness.

Since returning, I've thought a lot about that community of women. Of course, a trip lasting two weeks is hardly enough time for me to claim to really know and understand the community; all I can do is share what I observed. Overall, I think the role of women in their communities — be it in Tibet or Hong Kong or any number of other places — doesn't change. Women are the pillars of the home, nurturing, caring for, and catering to their loved ones, in addition to acting as breadwinners by working in the fields or holding industrial jobs.

I think the difference between that Tibetan community and mine is in the digital distance. The Tibetan women seemed to operate in their immediate physical environment. They cooked together, fetched water together, cleaned sheep's skin together by the riverside, and often belonged to one extended family. In my society, an individual's support network can be thousands of miles away. I'm in constant contact via the telephone, the Internet, and email with my sister in Paris, my friend in New York, and my mom in Malaysia. We are connected emotionally and spiritually but not physically anymore. That group of Tibetan women was connected through day-to-day living; they were physically close, while women like me are connected to our wider support group digitally over a great distance.

YEE-MING TAN • MALAYSIA

Yee-Ming Tan's educational background includes studies in Malaysia and Australia, as well as New Zealand, where she obtained a bachelor of arts degree in linguistics and international relations from Victoria University of Wellington. A conventional corporate career provided the opportunity for her to live in Singapore, Malaysia, Indonesia, and Hong Kong. In 2001 she began to devote time to the pursuit of creativity and artistic expression through the process of pottery making. She is the director of Third Thinking, a corporate culture consultancy.

ABOVE AND LEFT *The Women of Mount Kailash* series

The Karateginskaya community, situated on the outskirts of Dushanbe, suffered a lot during our civil war and is still considered a conflict area. This hilly place is like a deserted island, forgotten by everybody and even by God, women say to us. Looking at the faces of our women, one cannot even think that these fragile women have experienced so many tragedies. If someone would like to write a bestseller or a top-box-office movie about the world's strongest women, then they would have to come to Karateginskaya!

Our women especially suffered during the war, and so they value peace strongly. The war made them feel powerless, and being women in a traditional Muslim community only contributes to this feeling. You can imagine women whose husbands died or left for Russia to earn money outside of the country. The fear of being alone and without means to survive forced some of these women to be second or third wives [a legally ambiguous status wherein these women, as well as any children born of the marriages, are deprived of any formal rights].

But the more these women learn, the more they are enlightened and aware of things around and outside their small world. They are akin to gardens watered after a long drought: now their minds are awakening after a long sleep, growing and flowering as they absorb the knowledge provided. Our women try to make positive changes and create a better community for themselves and their children. They say, "The world is so beautiful because of our children-flowers." And this is the best motive for women in the Karateginskaya community.

DILRABO INOMOVA • TAJIKISTAN

Dilrabo Inomova was born in Tajikistan and lives and works in Dushanbe, a city that suffered greatly during her country's civil war and is still tormented with severe poverty and conflict. Dilrabo works for a women's project on behalf of a nonprofit organization called Counterpart Tajikistan, which encourages women to feel spiritual and physical satisfaction and to use it to engender happiness and enlightenment in their children.

LEFT AND ABOVE *Photos of our women's group from Karateginskaya Ulitsa*

This black-and-white portrait series began out of my frustration with the lack of positive images of queer women in both the mainstream and gay media. The photos were never anything I could relate to, and the women they portrayed were not the women I saw in my social and political circles. This portrait series is intended to portray a portion of the community that I believe deserves to be seen. Queer women are diverse and multifaceted, they come from all walks of life, and they possess many different kinds of beauty. These images push boundaries and break stereotypes without being inherently threatening.

ANH ÐÀO KOLBE • USA / VIETNAM

Born somewhere outside Saigon, Vietnam, Anh Ðào Kolbe came to the United States in 1972 when she was six months old. Her adoptive mother found her at An Lac Orphanage in Saigon, the orphanage from which over 220 Vietnamese children were rescued and taken to the United States. She went on to live with her Greek and German parents in Qatar and later in the Sultanate of Oman. After schooling in Britain she returned to the United States (more specifically, to Boston) for college. It was only after her graduation that she began to take the photographs that would make her the unofficial photographer of Boston's queer community.

ABOVE LEFT *Raquel Evita Saraswati-Seidel* ABOVE RIGHT *Salua Shabazz* RIGHT *Jill Paolini*

Profeta Gentileza (The Prophet of Kindness)

From the 1960s until recently, an enigmatic man circulated throughout Rio de Janeiro, triggering people's curiosity. He was an old man with the appearance of a biblical prophet: he had a long white beard, a long tunic, and Franciscan-style sandals, and he carried in his hands two tablets of written prophecies, like those of Moses. He approached people who passed in cars and on sidewalks, but he didn't ask for anything; instead, he offered them flowers, compassion, and words of love. The man became known as Profeta Gentileza (the Prophet of Kindness).

Part of his preaching consisted of writing his messages on the pillars of Viaduto do Cajú, a big viaduct here in Rio. That way, in the middle of the confusion, indifference, selfishness, and violence of the big city, all passersby could read on that giant urban display sentences such as:

KINDNESS GENERATES KINDNESS;

DON'T USE PROBLEMS, DON'T USE POVERTY, USE LOVE; and even

KINDNESS IS THE MEDICINE FOR ALL DISEASES.

When I was still a child it was incredible and fascinating for me to cross paths with this man. I remember that I used to observe, with curious eyes, his writings on the pillars of the viaduct. Seeing his illustrations on a street in the big city filled me with a feeling of freedom and affection.

In 1997 I went to the viaduct with a friend of mine to introduce him to Gentileza's work. I then learned that his work no longer existed. After the prophet's death in 1996, his murals became orphans, without any kind of care. The murals deteriorated, and eventually the Rio de Janeiro Urban Cleaning Company covered them with a layer of gray paint.

That night, I was so shocked and sad that I wrote the song "Gentileza" (Kindness), which I later recorded on my album *Memórias, Crônicas e Declaraçaöes de Amor (Memories, Chronicles and Declarations of Love;* 2000). Soon after that, I learned of a local movement to recover the writings of Profeta Gentileza. Owing to the efforts of the nongovernmental organization Rio with Kindness and the personnel at a local university who started the movement, today Gentileza's work has been totally restored and returned to the people of Rio.

The subject of kindness is a universal one; it offers us a way of awakening from the attitudes of indifference that surround us in cities. What generates violence is the anonymity and loneliness we feel in the middle of a crowd.

Profeta Gentileza used to preach fraternal love; he urged people to devote their attention to others and to create intimacy with each other.

A prophet is somebody who lights up the people.

KINDNESS GENERATES KINDNESS.

Gentileza

They erased everything
They painted it all gray
The word on the wall
Was covered over with paint

They erased everything
They painted it all gray
All that was left on the wall
Was sadness and fresh paint

We who pass in a hurry
Through the streets of the city
Deserve to read the letters
And the words of Kindness
So I ask
You of the world
What is more intelligent
The book — or wisdom?

The world is a school
Life is a circus
Love is a word that liberates
So said the poet

[FROM THE ORIGINAL PORTUGUESE]

Apagaram tudo
Pintaram tudo de cinza
A palavra no muro
Ficou coberta de tinta

Apagaram tudo
Pintaram tudo de cinza
Só ficou no muro
Tristeza e tinta fresca

Nos que passamos apressados
Pelas ruas da cidade
Merecemos ler as letras
E as palavras de Gentileza
Por isso eu pergunto
A vocês no mundo
Se é mais inteligente
O livro ou a sabedoria

O mundo é uma escola
A vida é o circo
Amor palavra que liberta
Já dizia o profeta

MARISA MONTE • BRAZIL

One of Brazil's most popular musicians, Marisa Monte studied opera in Italy during her teenage years but returned to Rio de Janeiro to start a pop career that has gained her international recognition. Born in 1967, Marisa has been described as a "key architect to remodel and reform bossa nova." Samba rhythms often filled her childhood home because her father brought together musicians from the Portela School of Samba for jam sessions. Her mother loved jazz and blues, while Marisa listened to Brazilian pop.

ABOVE Lyrics to "Gentileza" from the album *Memórias, Crônicas e Declaraçaões de Amor (Memories, Chronicles and Declarations of Love)*

WORK

SANDRA BELLO · MEXICO

Sandra Bello was born in Mexico City in 1980 and lives in Tijuana, Baja California, Mexico. She has a bachelor's degree in communications from the Autonomous University of Baja California (UABC) and a degree in photography from the Center for the Image at UABC. She is a member of the YonkeART promotion/production company and the multidisciplinary collective URBANA.

LEFT From the *Prod* series

Where Are America's Family Values?
[Originally published in *Glamour* magazine, November 2002]

Confession: this article was due a long time ago. But while I was writing it, a legal case I was working on blew up, the babysitter went on vacation, and both of my kids came down with stomach flu. This cacophony of conflicting demands put me in good company with the army of bleary-eyed working mothers who lurch between briefings and diapers, conference calls and games of peekaboo, the watercooler and the bottle warmer.

It's a big army, some twenty-five million strong, each of us struggling in our own unique way to bring a little order to the chaos. It's a fantastic feat that many American mothers accomplish every day. But instead of support and solutions, we get finger-wagging, finger-pointing, and sometimes, it seems, just the finger.

The dissing of American working moms starts at birth: ours is one of only two major industrialized nations without paid maternity leave (Australia is the other). In England, you get eighteen weeks of it; in Hungary, twenty-four. Compare this to our government's guarantee of a measly twelve weeks of unpaid leave if you work for a company of fifty or more people, and you get the picture. Worse still is the lack of national investment in affordable day care, resulting in heart-wrenching conflicts for those who can't afford to lose their jobs or to pay for the care their kids need.

Why, in a nation like ours, is it so hair-raising for a woman to combine children and career? The reality is that more than 70 percent of American women with school-age children work outside the home. For women like me, and I know how lucky I am, it's a choice that's made easier by a supportive spouse, solid child care, and a flexible workplace. I work because I love the law, I love my independence, and, perhaps most important, I have a boss who lets me work part-time. But many women don't have that option: they work under difficult circumstances in order to survive, and they do it without society's help.

Watching my son put Elmo down for a nap may in fact be worth not making law partner. It's a trade-off I can live with. (My law firm has been extraordinarily kind to me, but the reality is that private-practice lawyers are evaluated at least in part by the hours they log. An ambitious associate is rarely home on the weekend, much less by dinnertime on weekdays. I work three days a week and am home by 7 P.M.) But almost every working mother I know feels pulled in a direction other than the one she's chosen. When I'm with my kids, I need to keep myself from checking email constantly (anyone who has cleaned baby spit-up out of a keyboard knows whereof I speak). When I finally show up at the office on four hours of sleep, breast pump in tow and hopefully without too many wet Cheerios stuck to my back, I sometimes need to take a few deep breaths and remind myself that I'm a lawyer, not a Teletubby.

But even when a working mom manages to enjoy a moment of satisfaction and equilibrium, there will always be a member of the Women's Identity

KARENNA GORE SCHIFF • USA

Karenna Gore Schiff works on behalf of children's rights and well-being in New York City. She was formerly an attorney at Simpson Thacher & Bartlett. Karenna is perhaps best known for the electrifying speech she gave in 2000 in support of her father's U.S. presidential campaign. She is the author of *Lighting the Way: Nine Women Who Shaped America* (Miramax, 2006).

Patrol ready to weigh in. Cousins, neighbors, random people in the elevator — everybody has an opinion. "Kids need their mom at home at that age!" countless people have scolded me. And then, looking at me like I'm the shoe bomber, "How can you leave those little faces in the morning?"

Even my stay-at-home-mom friends aren't immune to criticism. People talk down to them, ask if they have any ambition, and simply don't recognize the amount of skill it takes to raise children.

Instead of giving women grief for the choices they make, let's try creating a better menu of choices: full-time, part-time, flextime, time off, for all parents. Why do we hold our government accountable for providing safe streets, good libraries, and efficient transportation, yet not decent before-school and after-school programs? Why is it so difficult for parents to take time off or to work part-time? Why do we pay child-care workers (who earn about $16,350 annually) less than pet sitters ($17,600)?

Rather than questioning the choices of women who are working hard to raise kids and pay bills, let's start questioning the choices of our lawmakers. Don't the people raising the next generation of Americans deserve resources comparable to those being allocated to the people developing the next generation of weapons? Yet the administration cut the funds for the Child Care and Development Block Grants, the main source of help for those who cannot afford quality child care. We should also consider expanding the approach of the Family and Medical Leave Act of 1993 to cover smaller businesses, provide more time off, and perhaps offer some paid maternity leave. Why not explore incentives to encourage employers to provide flextime and on-site day care?

As I accidentally pulled a pacifier out of my purse during a meeting the other day, I was struck again by how difficult it can be to check our home lives at the office door. I am privileged not to have to, but millions of working moms fight daily battles for time, money, and peace of mind.

Since the 2001 terrorist attacks in the United States, there has been a lot of talk about our nation coming together to lend a hand to those in need. Let's do that on behalf of all the parents who are trying to raise kids and not tear their hair out in the process. It doesn't matter if you're Marge Simpson, Wonder Woman, or a confirmed bachelorette; we can all raise a juice box, a briefcase, or a martini glass to that kind of change!

Nevine leaves her family's home at eight-thirty every morning to go to her office at a major Cairo construction site. Magda comes to work at Nevine's house at about ten o'clock A.M. She finishes work and leaves the house at about four-thirty P.M. Nevine goes home at five o'clock. The two women move within the confines of the same domestic space at different times of the day, hardly ever crossing paths.

For Nevine, her home is a place to unwind after long, stressful days at work in a male-dominated environment. For Magda, working as a maid (a profession stigmatized by society) in Nevine's home is just a means to support her large family of six. Their paths are divergent. Being women they have a lot in common, but they share more with women from their own economic backgrounds across the East/West divide than they do with each other.

The photographs here are of the everyday, the mundane, the not so memorable moments. With an almost boring quality about them, these images of domestic routine try to break through notions of exoticism and the difference of the other.

HALA EL KOUSSY • EGYPT

Born in 1974 and educated in Cairo, Hala El Koussy has worked as a commercial photographer and a part-time photography teacher at the American University in Cairo since 1998. Since 2000 she has developed and exhibited her own projects, often on the subject of (mis)communication and the politics of food. Her work has been exhibited in Cairo, Italy, and the United Kingdom.

ABOVE AND RIGHT *Magda and Nevine: Two Women from Egypt*

Letter to Stella

Mahal kong Stella,

Kumusta ka na? Kumusta na ang buhay diyan sa Canada? Nabanggit mo sa iyong huling sulat na mahirap ang buhay diyan, lalo na sa simula ng inyong buhay mag-asawa. Alam ko ang iyong nadarama. Marahil, pareho lang siguro ang mga paghihirap na ating nararanasan.

[FROM THE ORIGINAL TAGALOG]

My dear Stella,

How are you? How is life in Canada? In your last letter you mentioned that life is difficult there, especially at the start of your married life. I know the feeling. We are probably experiencing similar hardships.

You are lucky to be where you are. As you know, so many of our people here dream of going to Canada, the United States, the United Kingdom, Japan, and other countries. So many women pay large sums of money to leave in search of brighter futures, sometimes even illegally. Some of these women look for men to marry them, something they can't be blamed for, because life is so difficult here. Others take on any kind of work just to be able to earn a living. There are fortunate ones who get decent and respectable jobs. So don't give up — you'll find work, especially since you are in Canada legally.

There are different stories to tell about people we knew and grew up with. Remember my cousin Ella? She finished studying to become a doctor here, only to start all over again to become a nurse, as she heard that nurses in the West earn big salaries. It is an honorable profession, but her aunts can't understand why she had to do what she did. I hear she's in London now.

Then there's Julia, the daughter of a neighbor in Mariveles. Julia is a teacher in Texas now and reportedly has a huge house. Her older sister used to work in Hong Kong as a domestic helper.

Remember Lea, the basketball team's muse? She once invited me to apply with her to work in Japan. The last time I saw her, she was buying a plane ticket to Tokyo. Remember how our classmates used to laugh at her because she was such a stiff and graceless dancer? And she can't sing either. I don't know. I guess one just needs determination.

I still work as a cashier at a department store. Thank God, I've finally become a regular employee after years of working there. Lately, there have been a lot of strikes in our company because the owner refuses to pay fair wages. As much as I would like to join these strikes, my responsibilities to my family keep me from doing so. And even if I wanted to look for another job (because I do have a degree in management) it would be hard to find one, regardless of my education.

I myself am responsible for the tuition for Utoy, my youngest brother, a sophomore at a computer college, as well as that of my oldest sister Gina's children. She is out of work and has a useless husband who likes to gamble. They fight all the time, and he's even hurt her once. They survive on her earnings from selling rice cakes. Fortunately, the sibling after me, a new graduate, has already started working. She was hired by a customer-service call center in Ortigas. Classy, huh? There are a lot of these companies here now. They hire mostly women, up to 90 percent.

The trouble with her, though, is that she's too capricious and extravagant. You know how that is. Teenagers nowadays are too much like sheep and always have to be in style. The problem is that styles change so fast that it's expensive to keep up. In our time, there were no cell phones; computers only had black screens with green letters; and watching a movie at Shoemart was the only pastime we knew. Nowadays, women are up to all kinds of new things.

ESTRELLA SANTOS • PHILIPPINES

Estrella Santos is the pen name of a young woman from the Philippines. This letter is a fictional adaptation of a letter written to a young Filipino immigrant in Canada by an old friend. Still in the home country, the writer of the letter watches as ever more young women leave the Philippines with hopes of a more prosperous future abroad.

What used to be exclusively male events have now become female activities — things engaged in by "yuppies," as the young people here now like to call themselves — places like *Malate* bars where you get dressed up and go to see and be seen, air-conditioned pool halls, cybercafes, which are addictive even to the computer illiterate who go there to "chat," and coffeehouses with expensive coffee.

This is all for now. I have to go and watch my favorite *telenovela,* all the rage nowadays on TV.

Take care always.

Your friend,
Erlinda

P.S. I'm still waiting for a husband. Gabriel and I broke up because I caught him dating another girl. There are still three of us unmarried girls in our group of friends. We're always bridesmaids or sponsors but never the brides at weddings. My mother is rushing me to get married, as she says I might not be able to have a child or won't find anyone because I'll be over thirty.

Overheard During a Day's Work

[The following are remarks that Eliza has heard while working as a model.]

Shit, should I say twenty-five or twenty? . . . No, too young. Maybe twenty-two. Oh hell, it's Seventeen magazine . . . I'm eighteen today.

All right, elongate the neck, bend your arms because I see a little flab, extend your jaw, relax your lip, more hip, stronger eyes but not that strong, a little soft with the fingers, you're losing the neck, slouch but remain on the inhale . . . just be yourself.

Honey, if only you were three inches taller and ten years younger.

Sorry, the clients decided not to go ethnic with this campaign.

The music video part is for the lounge ho number one. It pays gummy bear rate and kills your character in twelve hours.

Models are so damn lucky . . . as long as all 1,352 of them can book one of the thirty jobs available, so they can quit that waitressing gig at the age of twenty-nine and retire a millionaire, or better yet, marry one!

Do you mind taking off your top? I'm French, so tits don't matter, baby.

ELIZA ESCAÑO • PHILIPPINES

Eliza Escaño, a native of the Philippines, is a writer residing in Los Angeles. After graduating with a degree in journalism, she worked in public relations for three years before being scouted by a modeling agency one night at a dance club. Since then, she has done campaigns and commercials for major corporations and has shot with renowned photographers, including Marc Baptiste and David La Chapelle.

NASRA ABUBAKAR • SOMALIA

Nasra Abubakar (on the left in the photograph) is from Somalia and lives in Nairobi, Kenya, where she and her husband are raising their son. She studied armed conflict at the University of Nairobi and works as a journalist.

My generation of women is called the unmanageable ones because we are working mothers who are trying our best to be independent.

I am different from my mother because she was a camel girl, meaning when she was young she took care of camels in the forest. Camel milk is free of sugar and fat and full of calcium. This makes anyone who is brought up drinking camel milk strong-boned. Those who care for camels also emerge as very good wrestlers. Because of her endurance and practice, my mother became an extraordinary wrestler herself. She was the best wrestler of her time; she actually had no equal, and men dreaded wrestling her. My mother never wrestled with us kids, and she never beat us. She was very kind and forgiving, and neighbors always complained that she was too lenient. But when she wanted something done she had a look that said, "You would rather do what I want you to." The things she wanted us to do included washing ourselves, wearing clean clothes, having afternoon naps when not going to school, and in my case, washing my hair twice or thrice a week. We were to wake up early in the morning to prepare for school, and we were also to do our homework. My mother never went to school herself, but she wanted us to get the best education we could.

I went to school and didn't have to take care of animals. My mother would never have dreamt of going to university, but I earned a diploma in armed conflict at the University of Nairobi.

About my husband. We fell in love and dated for almost three years before we got married. He is young, shy, handsome, kind, and gentle. He never raises his voice, and we have never fought. Of course we disagree, but we try to sort out our differences without annoying each other. On the other hand, I am very talkative compared with him; I do all the talking and he does most of the listening. Before we got married he was very quiet, but I have taught him to talk things out. We cope perfectly.

Of course, I am not so very different from other wives in my community. I have to wake up early, make breakfast, and prepare my husband's bath and his clothes, making sure he is well fed, bathed, and dressed. After work no matter what, I have to come home before him, cook a fresh, warm dinner, prepare his bedding and his bath, and do the rest of the chores.

Do not forget, I also have a baby who needs my care and attention. With few exceptions, husbands in my community don't change diapers or bathe babies. Well, I am a bit lucky because my husband loves our baby and helps me hold him at night, but he can't help me during the day, so we have to hire a nanny.

My challenge today with my fellow women is to see that Somali women and girls are given equal chances at all levels of education and participation in social events, even politics.

Traditional woven textiles *(Kain tenunan Brunei)* are produced by local women in Brunei. These textiles play important roles in the community; they serve as the basis of ceremonial costumes and also represent a source of income. Cloth weaving has traditionally been an inherited skill, especially among the Brunei Malay residing in Kampala Ayer (villages of houses built on stilts at the Brunei River), where older female siblings teach the younger ones their skills and expertise. The women usually perform their weaving activities at home after they have finished their household chores. However, there are also women who do not weave merely as a part-time activity but accept orders from clients and entrepreneurs. Cloth weaving provides additional income for women to improve their standard of living. Hence, women play a prominent part in contributing to the household economy.

SITI NORKHALBI HAJI WAHSALFELAH • BRUNEI DARUSSALAM

Siti Norkhalbi Haji Wahsalfelah is a lecturer at the University of Brunei Darussalam and recently completed a doctorate in anthropology and sociology at the University of Western Australia. Her passion for locally produced, traditional woven textiles has led her to research the subject; her doctoral work explores the process of the consumption of traditional woven cloths and the relationship between the expression and the construction of identity in Brunei Darussalam.

ABOVE *The Cultural Heritage of Brunei Darussalam: The Traditional Woven Textile*

Domestic Weave reflects the multiple roles of a young woman in an urban household. Woven around the central figure are women in different situations. While one is dutifully performing the chores of the kitchen surrounded by earthenware pickle jars, the other is at work being an independent breadwinner.

Women of my generation, who live in cities as I do, often find themselves under surveillance from the culture police. Although women in urban households are offered higher education, they are not always offered their choice of the future thereafter. I believe the nationwide campaign to educate the "girl-child" in India has been one of the main reasons for the change in the social status of women of my generation. Rural movements like Amul, a large cooperative dairy in the state of Gujarat, and other such organizations have brought a sense of financial independence among young women in villages. Many women of my generation recognize the choices they have in matters of marriage and childbearing, and they dare to acknowledge these choices in spite of social and religious pressures. Very few members of my mother's and grandmother's generations were offered these choices, and very few were educated.

I believe that women in my generation are privileged to have the chance to pursue education and a career and choose our own social status. However, modernization and global commercialization have brought many outside, Western influences. Are we going to be able to hold on to our past and pass it on to the next generation as our mothers did?

This becomes my concern when my child does not know the significance of some positive beliefs and religion. It becomes my concern when my child does not know his history, and the past has lost its value. Is the modern Indian woman cutting the umbilical cord?

HEERAL TRIVEDI • INDIA

Heeral Trivedi is an artist whose work reflects the young urban Indian woman. Her works explore the choices available to women of her generation and the need to recognize these choices as every woman's right.

ABOVE *Shelved I* and *II* **RIGHT** *Domestic Weave*

OMOTOYOSI ODUNSI • NIGERIA

Omotoyosi Odunsi, or Toyosi for short, was born in Lagos, Nigeria. She graduated with a degree in visual communication from the University of Leicester, England, and works as a photographer.

RIGHT AND FOLLOWING PAGES *Baby Women* series

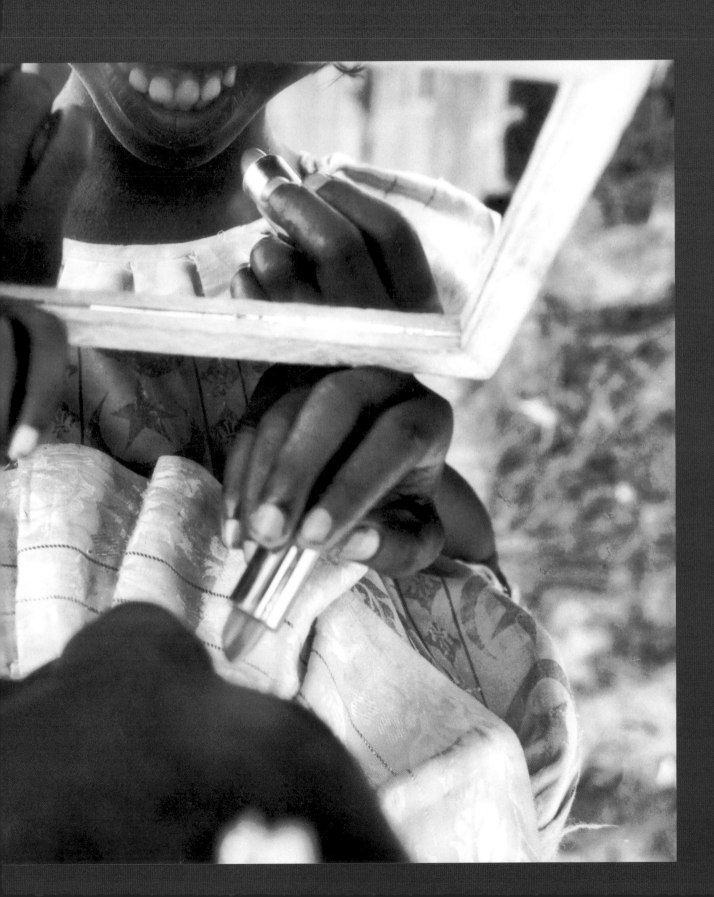

I see far too many baby women on the streets of Lagos, begging and selling everything, from cola at sixty naira a bottle to their bodies at one hundred naira a trick. These photographs are of one young woman whom I have been fortunate enough to photograph. At eleven years old, Khadija lives with her dad, her extremely young mother, and three younger sisters whom she looks after on a daily basis. She does not go to school. As an *okada* (bike taxi) rider, her father makes enough money to feed them, and her mother runs a small shop that doubles as their home. Most likely, Khadija will be married in the next three years and will be a mother in fewer than five. Her family loves her, and she does not go hungry, but she is one of the really lucky ones. There are millions of young girls like Khadija who have to play the role of mother to their siblings at a tender age but who do not have careers or the love or support of their parents.

POWER

CHRISTINE LUKSZA-PARAVICINI • USA

In 1997 Christine Luksza-Paravicini found herself inspired by the pregnant body as she witnessed her own body transform during her first pregnancy. In her work she wants to expose the huge bellies, enlarged breasts, and even swollen thighs, to display and exhibit the curious features the pregnant body temporarily holds.

LEFT *Lilypads*

I HAD DONE IT. Ever since I was a little girl running around in Mackay in northern Queensland, Australia, I had dreamt of this moment. At Homebush Stadium on September 25, 2000, I achieved my lifelong goal of winning an Olympic gold medal. And to do so in Australia in front of II2,000 people screaming my name — it was magical.

You cannot imagine my sense of relief at crossing the finish line. It was like I had been trapped in a sauna and suddenly the door had been flung open. This photo was taken on my victory lap. I hadn't done one since the 1994 Commonwealth Games, where I had been criticized in some quarters for flying the Aboriginal flag, so this time I made sure that I picked up both the Aboriginal and the Australian flags that the crowd had thrown onto the ground by the finish line. I tied them together and put them around my neck and tried to make my way around the track without bumping into all the photographers around me. The crowd was going crazy, and music was pumping out around the stadium — I couldn't believe I had made so many people so happy.

I'm so proud of who I am and where I'm from, and to me, this photo brings it all together perfectly. Pure joy, pride, and relief all mixed together. I may feel like just a little black girl who can run fast, but I'm also a woman who followed her heart and achieved her childhood dream. I am honored that I was able to share my golden moment not only with everyone in the stadium that night, but also with Australia, and with my people.

CATHY FREEMAN • AUSTRALIA

Cathy Freeman, who was born in Mackay, Australia, in 1973, discovered her passion for running at age five. That passion led her to the Olympic cauldron, which she lit to open the 2000 Olympic Games in Sydney. During the ensuing track and field competition, she won the women's four-hundred-meter race, becoming the first Aboriginal athlete to take home an Olympic gold medal. Cathy can run one hundred meters in 11.24 seconds, and she trains nearly six hours a day. She also is engaged in indigenous issues, enjoys dancing, and loves spending time with her family, her friends, and her two cats, Billy and Jazz.

MARAMA DAVIDSON • NEW ZEALAND

Marama Davidson is a Mäori woman from Aotearoa (the Mäori name for New Zealand), who lives with her husband, Paul, and two daughters. She works full-time for the New Zealand Human Rights Commission as an educator. Her father, Rawiri Paratene, is a prominent Mäori actor and activist, who is well known internationally, most recently for his role as the father in the film *Whale Rider*. Marama was born into the turbulent 1970s while her teenage parents passionately worked for the Mäori cause of reclaiming their rights to their land, language, and culture — a time that Marama refers to in the story of what has shaped her as a young woman.

This Is Me

I am the product of two young lovers who met while on a protest march for land. They were teenagers then, and not long after, I was born. To be precise, my parents met while camped outside the steps of Parliament in Wellington, Aotearoa. Their world, I am told, was a bit different from mine.

The story goes that my mother actually turned up at Parliament with another man, who is also a prominent pro-Mäori figure today. But she left with my father. And for that I do not complain. My parents went on to get married and have two more children.

This all happened in the 1970s; the 1970s and 1980s in Aotearoa were turbulent in terms of race relations between Mäori and *päkeha* [New Zealanders of British/European descent]. There was this thing called the Te Tiriti O Waitangi [the Treaty of Waitangi], an agreement between the British Crown royalty and the Mäori people signed in 1840 — it was going to protect our people from spiritual death. My parents, and many other Mäori, just wanted the government to honor it.

So they marched and shouted. They got thrown off rugby fields and into jails for protesting South African apartheid. They "bared all" to insult the visiting (British) Crown royalty. They fought violently with *päkeha* university students who denigrated Mäori cultural traditions. They squatted on supposed "Crown land" until the police physically removed them from it. And they physically walked the length of the North Island to remind us of the promises of the treaty.

As a child I watched my parents fight with our landlord, and with the ears of a babe I heard the landlord cry, "Bloody Mäoris, you should all go back to Bastion Point!" As an infant I watched my mummy and daddy get beaten up by police, all the while being called "black bastards." Later, the police complaints department said "Complaint dismissed."

My children have not seen anything like that in their upbringing. Why? It is because my time is different. It is because I am different. It is because the feelings are different. It is not because things are better.

I can never speak for all Mäori, not even for all Mäori women. My stories are about me, and through them will emerge the different colors of the many *käkahu* [cloaks] I wear: that of Mäori, that of *wähine* [female], that of mother, that of wife, that of aspiring career woman, and that of friend. But one *käkahu* I wear vigorously is that of a young Mäori woman choosing to live in the city. It is a *käkahu* which saw me growing up all over Aotearoa and attending a range of schools.

I attended the all-*päkeha* South Island city schools ("Say a Mouwry word for us!"), the small rural Mäori area schools, the "elite" urban Mäori girls' boarding school, and finally the huge city high schools hosting many different ethnicities and races. This *käkahu* was all-encompassing and offered me beautiful — if sometimes cruelly honest — experiences.

I would like to remember two women who helped weave my spiritual *käkahu*. The first is my nanny (grandmother), Patricia Charlotte Broughton. I was the first *moko* [grandchild] to come into her life, and I was born on the twenty-fifth wedding anniversary of her and Papa (my grandfather). She has been dead for fifteen years, and I miss her like she left us yesterday. I was only a young girl when

Marama Davidson with her father, 1973

continued

she passed away and joined my papa, leaving our lives, but I feel her *wairua* [spirit] eternally. She is inside me more than my own heart is.

When her *mokopuna* [grandchildren] were born she would pull our flat noses with her fingers to try and make them pointier — like the *pākeha* ones. Her efforts were in vain because here we all are today with the flattest noses ever! When she would visit *pākeha* people she would put on bright red lipstick and purse her lips in a way that would make them smaller — like *pākeha* ones. My siblings and I owe our gloriously large, juicy lips to her.

My nanny was a fluent and eloquent speaker of my native language, *te reo Māori*, and also of English. Her faith in the Catholic Church was the pinnacle in her way of life. She was the best cook ever, and she loved her *mokopuna* like there was no tomorrow. She was fierce in her protection of her *whānau* [family]; I am sharply reminded of the time when she took me to her work to help out and her boss refused to pay me. There is no anger like that of a nanny for her unfairly treated grandchild. Needless to say, in the end I received good pay for that day.

Nanny loved my father and her other children so much that she cut the cords that connected them to their spiritual homeland in the rural countryside and took them to receive the best of the *pākeha* world in the city. For the most part my father flourished, but he would inevitably feel a sense of disconnection. . . .

And so would my mother. She would yearn to be Māori but not always know how, being a born-and-bred Wellingtonian. My mother — Hanakawhi Alexandra Paraone Nepe-Fox — also weaves herself through the *kākahu* that protects and nourishes me. As a woman raising a family, I begin to fully appreciate her strength, her dignity, her honesty, and her wisdom. My father and mother felt the loss that many of their cohorts did — the loss of language, the loss of land, the loss of *mana* [self-worth]. Spiritual death seemed too close to them.

I am thankful for their radical antics that I spoke of earlier — I face no such spiritual death. But I face things my parents and grandparents never did as young people trying to negotiate their way in this new world.

The Aotearoa I live in has been forced to acknowledge the status of Māori culture and the promises of its protection made under the Treaty of Waitangi. Today I can access any number of Māori educational learning services, from *Kohanga Reo* [nursery] for my babies to *wānanga* [institutions] or universities to receive tertiary qualifications. More career opportunities are available to me as a speaker of *te reo Māori* than as a Māori who cannot "talk the talk." Today I am called on in my central city corporate office building for my knowledge and experience in Māori ceremonial welcome, my skill in *karanga* [a traditional performance], and my ability to perform *waiata* [chanting].

Indeed, my mates and I constantly compete with each other on how "Māori Māori" we have managed to become. It comes down to the number of Māori art pieces on our walls, the size of the *taonga* [traditional pendant] around our necks, the number of syllables we've managed to include in our child's Māori name, how long we can stand up and *mihi* [praise] in Māori without faltering, and how many items of clothing we own with a Māori design on them. We are staunchly proud of who we are, while all too well aware of the "white lash" that has accompanied the rise of Māori culture within New Zealand society.

Not as many landlords today are telling us to "Go back to Bastion Point," and not as many police are bashing us and calling us "black bastards," but the fear and insecurity of many are more underlying, and more dangerous. I choose to ignore these underlying tones, be it a lean towards blissful ignorance or the realization that some people are too far gone for me to worry about. My parents faced blatant opposition, outright hatred, violence, and mass racism. These things still exist today but in ways far more institutionalized than ever.

But as I said, I choose to ignore that fact.

I instead make good use of the opportunities that are available to me as a young Mäori woman. I took part in a four-week-long kayaking voyage that retraced the traditional waterways of my *tü-puna* [ancestors]. I have been on climbing expeditions to summit snowy Tongariro and Ngauruhoe mountains. I modeled in the Pasifika Fashion Show, which has become a first-class professional performance. I have scaled cliffs in rock climbing expeditions to Northland and Waikato. I embarked on study at the Auckland University as a teenage mother. I work with pride and passion at the Human Rights Commission, where I strive to affect the lives of people every day. I am proud of all of that.

The negative numbers that show themselves in the social, economic, and cultural reports concerning the Mäori people mean little to me. I am not in those numbers; they do not define who I am or who my people are. They are only guidelines for where my work lies, but I don't need reports to tell me that.

One thing that does define me, though, is the work of my weavers; those who have contributed to the making of my spiritual *käkahu*. Most important, they are my nanny, my mother, and my father.

I began this account by telling about my *whakapapa* [genealogy], so I find it appropriate to finish with reference to it also. Specifically, I want to talk about my mother. With all the mountains and rivers I have conquered, my university degree, my fashion modeling achievements, my meaningful and rewarding career, and my vast worldly experiences, I can only hope to reflect some of the wondrous woman that is my mother. With none of the above to put next to her name, she is mum, wife, and grandmother extraordinaire and my eternal source of wisdom, knowledge, and soul food. She needs nothing but herself to be great, and she has guided me through my life as a Mäori woman. As a shaper of people she is the most fantastic artist I know, carving

within me a love for my *whänau* [birthplace], *hapü* [clan], and *iwi* [community]. I am bound by this love and will slowly make whatever mark I have so that the world may realize it.

Na reira, nga mihi nui ki a koutou, tënä koutou, tënä koutou, tënä tätou katoa. To that end, my warmest admiration and respect to all of you, and to all of us.

This is Me

Hikurangi is the mountain
Waiapü is the river
Ngäti Porou is the tribe

And on my father's side . . .

Te Ramaroa and Panguru are the mountains
Whirinaki and Hokianga are the rivers
Te Hikutu and Ngai Tupoto are the subtribes
Ngäpuhi and Te Rarawa are the tribes

Breath of life!  **[FROM THE ORIGINAL MÄORI]**

Ko Ahau Tënei

Ko Hikurangi te maunga
Ko Waiapü te awa
Ko Ngäti Porou te iwi

Ki te taha o töku päpa . . .

Ko Te Ramaroa me Panguru ngä maunga
Ko Whirinaki me Hokianga ngä awa
Ko Te Hikutu me Ngai Tupoto ngä hapü
Ko Ngäpuhi me Te Rarawa nga iwi

Tihei Mauriora!

Excerpt from Speech Presented at the World Economic Forum

Davos, Switzerland, 2003

It goes without saying that ours is a critical time, not simply in terms of global security or politics or economics. It is a critical time in terms of ideas — the basic ideas on which this century builds its promise, ideas like peace with justice, equal opportunity, and tolerance of others.

These values are goals, certainly — ideals to aim for in the best of worlds. But let me suggest that today peace, opportunity, and tolerance are more than goals; they are also resources, essential elements of our increasingly global system. They drive twenty-first-century success no less than energy or technology. In that sense, peace and opportunity and tolerance are not luxuries, not the final icing on the cake. They are the very bread of life, the fuel that is needed, right now, for a safe, free, and prosperous world.

So, we need to ask ourselves, As a global community, have we invested sufficiently in these resources? And most of all, what are we doing to build trust in our values, to make them something on which all people can rely?

To me, these questions are made very urgent by the "hope gap" that I have seen around the globe — the dangerous gulf between those people who really feel part of this new century and the many, far too many, who feel left behind. . . .

Think about a boy in the West Bank who powers on a computer and looks through a virtual window onto a world of peace and prosperity. Then he looks out his own window at barricades and violence and closed streets. And this goes on year after year. What's at risk for that child and other children, on both sides of this conflict, is trust that peace can ever be real. That is an attitude they will carry into adult life if we don't make a difference now.

Or think about a young girl in Afghanistan who can finally go to school after years of exclusion. Then the school-door slams shut because there are no funds for books or teachers or technology. What's at risk for this child, and many others, is real hope in the opportunity to share in this century. Again, that's an outlook that can shape their lives for years to come. . . .

People who are trapped by failed hopes can easily become disillusioned and cynical about values like peace and tolerance. And cynicism is contagious; it can also affect those looking from the outside in and diminish their will to make ours a better world. Yet humanity's greatest message may be that contrary to the cynics, trust in core values does pay off.

This is something that we in Jordan really understand. We are a small country, resource-poor, hemmed in by some of the world's most bitter conflicts. Development, education, health, economic growth — all these are huge challenges. In today's climate, with the Palestinian-Israeli conflict raging to our west, and a potential war looming to our east, it might seem easy to write us off. Indeed, it might seem easy for Jordanians to be cynical about their prospects, to shift to low gear, to lay low, to put off our crucial reform plans until the political storms around us subside. Instead, under the leadership of His Majesty King Abdullah, we have pushed forward an accelerated model of achievement and excellence. We have decided to strengthen our trust in age-old values of hard work, peace, and equal opportunity. More importantly, we have decided not to throw in the towel, come what may.

This is the genius of Jordan, and it is beginning to pay off. We see that in economic growth — over 5 percent in 2002; we see that in all the leading indicators, such as productivity, cash reserves, and exports. But we also see it in terms of attitude and confidence. Allow me to quote a recent newsletter published by a leading investment bank in Jordan: "Investors at the Amman Stock Exchange (ASE)

QUEEN RANIA AL-ABDULLAH · JORDAN

Her Majesty Queen Rania Al-Abdullah (formerly Rania Al-Yasin) was born in Kuwait in 1970 to a notable Jordanian family of Palestinian origin. After her marriage to then-Prince Abdullah, Queen Rania channeled her energies into initiatives that aim to improve the lives of Jordanians from various sectors of society. As Queen Rania is First Lady, her activities encompass issues of national concern, including the environment, youth, human rights, tourism, and culture, among others.

still seem unfazed by political news, which hampered their activity in 2002, and are now trading quite enthusiastically."

Ours is a leadership that devotes all its energy to making hope real. And in my journeys around the world, I have seen that same spirit in many places. Especially here at Davos, I meet winners in every sphere, who have the gift of making their ideas and values come to life. I believe that we now have a challenge, and an opportunity, to help millions around the world make their hopes real.

One important challenge is to bring our values to bear on one of the worst "hope gaps" in the world: the gap between regions that have enjoyed the benefits of peace and those that are paying the terrible price of ongoing violence and conflict. If we are going to fuel new realities, we need to find a way to flow hope across this divide.

Today, just as a pipeline connects areas rich in resources like oil or water with areas that lack these essential resources, a "peace-line" is needed to bring the benefits of peace to regions in conflict. That means, for example, flowing more investment — or perhaps I should say, more creative investment — into war-tired communities. New public-private partnerships can be a seedbed to grow civil society. A global commitment to opening the school doors can open minds as well. And innovative outreach, like microfinance, can bring solutions to the street. In Kosovo, I visited communities being rebuilt by war survivors, many of them women, using loans as small as one hundred dollars. This work has the power to transform lives.

Perhaps most of all, a "peaceline" means streaming a new dialogue of tolerance and mutual respect, one that understands we all have a stake in the global system. The West–Islamic World dialogue that has begun at this Forum is a major contribution. . . .

The idea of a "peaceline" is just one way to think about the deep connections among us. Truly, global peace isn't something that we will get by turning on a tap. We will have to work for it, drill deep, and keep the ideas and hope flowing. The well of human creativity and capability is never empty. The resources of peace, of opportunity, of tolerance are there.

I learned that best from the life of my father-in-law, His Late Majesty, King Hussein. He reigned for forty-seven years and had basically seen it all — the rise and fall of nations, the dramatic shift in alliances, the demise of great leaders. He worked for peace for several decades. Every ounce of success was weighed down by tons of disappointments. He had every right to be cynical about the prospects of peace. Indeed, he would have been forgiven if he had relabeled cynicism and called it realism. But he chose not to.

In the last months of his life, the Arab-Israeli peace process had again stalled in violence. At that time, King Hussein was being treated for advanced cancer. Instinctively, he left the cancer unit and went back to work for peace at the Wye River Conference. He attended, if you recall, the White House ceremony announcing an agreement. He looked frail from his battle with cancer, but his eyes foretold a story of a moral passion that will live on long after his death.

And, indeed, ours is a better world because people can still trust his values. King Hussein taught me, and millions of others, that in the pursuit of basic values, such as peace and freedom, we can never fail. We just have to keep the hope alive, continue the dialogue, and top it all off with plenty of hard work.

Interview with Amina Lawal

In September 2003 I met Amina Lawal, an illiterate villager from northern Nigeria who was made famous in 2001 when an Islamic Shari'a court sentenced her to death by stoning for having a baby out of wedlock. At the time of our meeting, she was appealing the sentence and in a matter of weeks would be sitting before an appeals court to receive the judges' ruling.

I first met Amina at the house of her lawyer, Hauwa Ibrahim. The following day, she and her lawyer came to my fiancé's house for the interview. Amina brought her baby, who was then one year old.

Talking with Amina was difficult. We spoke different Nigerian languages, and she didn't speak English. She had gone to Koranic School, where she had memorized parts of the Koran and learned how to pray, but she hadn't had a secular education. Questions had to be simple; subordinate clauses confused her.

However, from our first meeting, I was struck by the air of peace and calm that surrounded Amina. She seemed gentle, self-effacing, and docile. During the interview, she spoke briefly and sometimes would not speak at all, preferring to let her lawyer, who had become like a second mother to her, speak for her.

Below is the interview, followed by my reflections on the experience.

Could you talk about your background, childhood, parents, and family?
[Amina's lawyer answers for her.] Amina is from a village called Kurami, in Katsina state. Her father, a farmer, died when she was young, and she grew up with her mother and stepfather. She has no formal education but went to Koranic School. She got married when she was thirteen or fourteen years old. She has three kids with her husband and was divorced a couple of days ago. Her oldest child is twelve years old.

What are your expectations for your life?
I leave my life to God.

What were your dreams when you were growing up?
We had no dreams. We were not brought up to think that we could dream.

Since the Shari'a case, how has your life changed?
My situation is not one that is accepted. People look at me when I go out. Even before the incident, I liked to stay at home and rarely went out. Now, with this, I go out even less.

What are your expectations now?
There are different types of expectations in life. Given my situation, I keep wondering, will I be killed?

What key things have you learned because of your recent experiences?
There is no space for me anywhere. At my age, I am not meant to be in my father's house but in my husband's house. When I stay with my parents, after a few days, they become fed up with me. It is not their fault, as their house is small. [Her lawyer uses her hands to show how small.]

What are your plans for after the case?
I just want to get married.

To whom?
God will provide.

Where will you live with him?
Wherever God sends him from.

Has any man shown interest in you recently?
Yes. There was a man who showed interest. My mother said he had to meet with my senior mother [the term by which her lawyer is known]. She [the lawyer] interviewed him and quickly found that the man thought I was receiving money from people outside. He was interested in the money.

Are you interested in going to school?
No. I prefer to get married.

HAFSAT ABIOLA • NIGERIA

Hafsat Abiola is the founder and director of the Kudirat Initiative for Democracy (KIND), which seeks to strengthen democracy in Nigeria. Her father, M. K. O. Abiola, won the country's 1993 presidential election, but the military annulled the election and incarcerated Abiola a year later. He died in prison, on the eve of his release. Hafsat's mother, Kudirat, a democracy leader, was assassinated in 1996 in the streets of Lagos. Hafsat travels around the world to speak about justice issues and writes articles featured in the international and Nigerian press.

How has your view of justice, religion, and others in your village changed?

I just want to leave others to God. Whoever thinks he is dispensing justice, I leave to God.

What would you say to other young women or girls in your community about what you have learned about how to live your life?

Who would I talk to? If I talked to the girls in my village, they would turn around and insult me.

Amina Lawal meets her legal team on March 25, 2003, at the Upper Sharia Court in Katsina, Nigeria.

My Reflections

"We had no dreams. We were not brought up to think that we could dream." Amina said that when I asked her what her dreams were when she was growing up. It seemed the logical question to ask as Amina, her lawyer, and I sat together.

Amina was clear about one thing: if her appeal was successful, she wanted to get married. Without conducting a survey, I think it's safe to say that getting married is the most popular dream among young women of my generation in Nigeria. It's difficult for it to be otherwise. Your parents and the friends of your parents pray for you to be married, and they do it in your presence, so there will be no confusion about their priorities for you.

In another facet of my life, I offer leadership programs for young women in Nigeria. One of the women in the inaugural class, Zainab, is remarkable because she rejected her family's arranged marriage. Zainab wants to be a doctor. Failing to convince her to get married instead, her parents went ahead with the wedding arrangements with her betrothed in Saudi Arabia and forced Zainab to go to Niger, the country north of Nigeria, to begin her long journey across the Sahara and the Red Sea to her husband. Zainab escaped and returned to Nigeria, where she found KIND; she is now working on her university entrance exams, still intent on becoming a doctor.

Zainab's aunt just had a baby a week ago, and she delivered the baby by herself. It isn't clear if this is the practice among her people or if the baby came too quickly and at a time when her family couldn't get her to the hospital. In any case, the baby girl was born feet first. It was a difficult delivery, and the baby died. I am looking forward to a time when Zainab will hold health seminars for women in her community so they can take care of themselves and their babies.

In the work I am doing, I realize that many women are still waiting for permission to be present, permission to make different choices and still be accepted by their community. When Amina said we were not told we could have dreams, she was speaking for herself, a poor, illiterate village woman. But she was also speaking for so many other women, women who are educated and seemingly accomplished but who are still expressing another's thoughts through their voice, seeing another's vision through their eyes.

Ultimately, imagining ourselves must be imagining ourselves authorized.

LAUREN BUSH • USA

Lauren Bush was born in 1984 in Texas and is the niece of U.S. President George W. Bush. Lauren has devoted her time to public service; she has done work on behalf of children's shelters, hospitals, women reentering the workforce, and various animal rights groups. She is currently a student at Princeton University and the Honorary Spokesperson for the World Food Program's Global Hunger Campaign.

Cambodian Diary

This is an excerpt from Lauren Bush's diary of her trip to Cambodia in September 2004. Lauren documented her experience traveling with a representative from the World Food Program (WFP) and interacting with the people of Cambodia.

Today is our last day in Cambodia. After meeting at the office of the charity organization Caritas, we drive for about an hour, going eventually from tarmac to bumpy dirt road to a village where families are getting HIV/AIDS counseling and care. A Caritas staff member checks on each family regularly to make sure they are getting enough food and medicine and have the transportation to go into town to get their meds.

The first family we visit is a beautiful couple, both of them with AIDS. None of their four children, they think, are infected. There is a fifth child on the way. The couple have recently started taking ARVs [anti-retroviral drugs] and seem fairly healthy. When we ask why they allowed a pregnancy to happen when both are infected, the wife replies that they forgot their birth control. They bring out a big jar filled with all the pills they take to stay healthy. Their kids are sitting by their sides, silently looking at the ground. If something happens to stop their parents from getting ARVs, then these little kids will lose both of their parents.

The next person we visit is a woman whose husband has just passed away from AIDS. Once her husband died, she tested positive. She has eight kids, all of whom live near her. Some are married and helping to support her. Her nineteen-year-old daughter is nine months pregnant. She is one of the most beautiful people I have ever seen. The mother explains that her daughter's boyfriend left once he found out she was pregnant. When we ask if her daughter has been tested for AIDS, the mother says that her daughter doesn't like needles. We explain that if the girl is positive and knows that before giving birth, she can save her child from being born with AIDS by getting a Caesarian section. Looking at this girl, who is absolutely radiant, I know that if she had been born in other circumstances, she would have the world at her feet. Here, she is pregnant, abandoned, and possibly infected with HIV, and she is younger than I am.

The last family we visit is a couple who both have AIDS. Their hut is also a small shop where they sell rice and noodles, fish, and other basic necessities. They have one little boy who is also infected. The woman did not know her husband had AIDS when they conceived their son. During our conversation, tears well up in her eyes. She says she is so angry with her husband that she will never forgive him. She cries for a few minutes. All the man can do is sit there ashamed, as their cute little boy bounces around energetically in the background.

Apparently most of the infected women contract the virus from their husbands, who have been sleeping around. The women then pass it on to their children unknowingly when they give birth. Then they are all trapped. Most of a woman's economic support comes from her husband. It is not like in America where people can just get divorced on a whim. Here, they are bound together with a deadly disease, living as outcasts in their society.

It is clear that were it not for organizations like WFP, the situation here would be hopeless and catastrophic. Instead, many who would have died are able to carry on, and this gives rise to hope for a healthy and happy future, especially for Cambodia's next generation.

MORGANA VARGAS LLOSA • PERU

Morgana Vargas Llosa is a photographer and the daughter of Mario Vargas Llosa, an eminent writer. With humanitarian compassion, Morgana has worked for organizations such as UNICEF, the United Nations, and ActionAid. While photographing the humanitarian tragedy in Kosovo, she felt protected behind the camera, allowing it to speak of life through its lens.

ABOVE *Women in Conflict — War in Kosovo*

War

When I think of how best to define my generation, these days one thing comes to mind: war. Sure, one could say reality TV or hip-hop music, as they have each had a distinctive impact on how we live, how we dress, and how we think (at least in the United States and much of the Western world). But I believe that the wars in which America is engaged in 2005 — whether ill-conceived or not — will shape who we will become.

I was born as the Vietnam War was nearing its end, and my concept of war as a child came from Hollywood films such as *Full Metal Jacket* and *Born on the Fourth of July.* Little did I know at the time that war would come to play a tremendous role in so many aspects of my life.

I always knew that I wanted to pursue journalism as a career, and I was fortunate enough to get a job as a reporter for a news program seen in schools across the country. However, I never imagined I would end up in Afghanistan covering its civil war during my freshman year of college. Afghanistan was a place that most Americans could barely identify on a map but one with which we were deeply enmeshed. To try to quell the spread of Communism, the United States pumped billions of dollars into Afghanistan during its ten-year war against the Soviets. With the help of U.S. aid and high-tech weapons, the Afghans were victorious. After the war, America pulled most of its resources out of that country, and the Afghans turned their weapons on each other. A brutal power struggle ensued that lasted for more than a decade and continues today. Many Afghans allege that the United States abandoned them after they fought a decade-long proxy war against the Soviet Union. Some charge that the United States allowed Afghanistan to devolve into civil war. Resentment for America ran high there at the time.

Stepping off the plane in Jalalabad, one of Afghanistan's major cities, was like entering the twilight zone. It was 1994, and the country had been in a constant state of war since 1979, when the Soviet Union first tried to conquer it. Hardly any buildings were intact; they had been bombed out over and over again. The remains of the standing structures were riddled with bullet holes. I was immediately surrounded by throngs of young boys fully armed with Kalashnikov assault rifles and bazookas. Some of the firearms were so hulking they dwarfed the boys carrying them. The only image to which I could compare these little warriors would be the Mongol warlords of the thirteenth century, but much younger and minus the decoration. I asked a few of them how old they were, and they returned absent stares; they had no idea.

All over the world, whenever I show up with camera crews, children with curious faces and jovial spirits relentlessly try to follow us around. But here, boys who looked no more than ten years old sat expressionless, waiting — as they had all of their lives — to fire their weapons and kill. Never before had I looked into the eyes of so many people and seen death. It was as if any one of them could have shot me right then and there and thought nothing of it.

LISA LING • USA

Lisa Ling is the host of *Explorer* on the National Geographic Channel and a regular contributor to the *Oprah Winfrey Show.* At age sixteen, the Northern California native auditioned for and was chosen to be one of four hosts of *Scratch,* a nationally syndicated teen magazine show out of Sacramento, California. By the time she was eighteen, Lisa had moved on to become one of the youngest reporters for Channel One News, a news channel for middle schools and high schools. While working more than forty hours a week for the news station, she attended the University of Southern California. Before the age of twenty-five, Lisa became Channel One News's senior war correspondent.

I distinctly remember thinking to myself at the time, What is going to happen to these boys and this country ten years from now? During the entire time I was there, I never saw one woman's face. What would become of a country in which young armed boys ran wild and women lived in the shadows even when they were in public?

It has been ten years since my first visit to Afghanistan, and the United States is once again engaged there. Only this time the United States is fighting its own war on Afghan soil — against extremists and the "terror" that they propagate. I often wonder whether the same boys I encountered ten years ago are now aiming their weapons and sentiments at the United States. What is more unnerving is that these days Afghanistan is only one place where young people are coming of age harboring disregard and disdain for America. In more than a decade of reporting overseas, I have witnessed support for my country rapidly erode. Since my first visit to Afghanistan, I have visited Iraq, Iran, Colombia, Nepal, and more than two dozen other countries. Many people in the United States don't realize that throughout the world tremendous numbers of disenfranchised people under the age of thirty are growing up feeling animosity towards Americans. It's frightening. I recently spent a couple of weeks in the Gaza Strip and had feelings similar to those I experienced ten years ago in Afghanistan. My worry, frankly, is less for my generation than for future generations, who will be inheriting the problems we face today. I certainly don't have the answer. However, I do think it might behoove us to start asking "Why?" more often.

One of the main reasons I wanted to work for National Geographic was because it is an organization that truly seeks to cover the world in a comprehensive way — and not just when there is catastrophe or war. Giving Americans more opportunities to learn about people of other cultures and how they live, rather than inciting hatred and animosity, is of immense importance to me. On a number of occasions during my travels, I was the first American some people had ever encountered. I have almost always been met with kindness and curiosity. After spending time and talking with people, I am convinced that most of them were left thinking, "She's not so bad." Well, neither were they.

I want a world where my inner-city students see education, not money, as a way out, where they can achieve more than what they see around the corner from their school. I want a world where twelve-year-olds see that living isn't about throwing punches but simply rolling with the punches. I want a world where my writers will keep writing and never be told to stop.

My Precious Ones in the Bronx

[A dialogue between a teacher and her students post-9/11]

Miss, I know you look like them but you're different
Your father? I don't know, it's different
You all've been living here

Miss, there's just too many of them comin' in
Too many
We've gots to be more careful now

Us, miss? I'm American but not really
You know
Do I look white to you?
I'm 100% Dominican but I'm from here
I live here
My parents, Miss? They're the same.
We go to the Dominican but that's just to visit

Miss, us all belong here
And I'm sorry them people be hatin' on you
But they be stupid and don't hear you talk
And don't know where you're from
They be dumb 'cuz your face don't look like you talk

American? Do we look white to you?
I am a Boriqua, and Tara is black, but we belong here
Why do they all keep coming?
This ain't no playground.
Everyone just keep comin' all up in here
Like it's Disney World
I wish I could go tell 'em Osama yo mama and get the
   hell out

Those ESL kids, Miss?
Well I guess they're ok.
I mean, they wear those head things
And other kids be sayin' some disrespectful shit to them
   but they seem okay.
They be real quiet anyway

But you still gotta wonder
Ms. Chowder said that one kid in that class just up
   and left
They say he moved to Canada but not really
He really moved back to Pakistan
Him and his whole family be Osama freaks and went
   back there for I don't know what.
And Ms. Chowder even said
So I'm sure it's true, Miss

And today I said nothing
Because today I am tired
And today is just today
Today
And so it goes and goes.

Miss, let's skip the lesson today and talk about this
   stuff more
We never get to talk as a class, Miss
Miss?
Miss?

NEELIMA REDDY • USA

Neelima Reddy is of Indian descent, but she was born and raised in Chicago and moved to New York City in 1994 to attend New York University. She is now teaching eighth-grade English in the Bronx while attending NYU's Graduate School of Education as a part-time student. Much of her work is drawn from and created for this diverse community of students.

PRUDENCE NOBANTU MABELE · SOUTH AFRICA

Prudence Nobantu Mabele is HIV-positive, a long-term survivor, and an advocate for people living with HIV. She is the founder and executive director of the Positive Women's Network based in Pretoria, South Africa. Prudence has worked in the HIV/AIDS field since 1992 and has written about women and AIDS in Africa for international foundations and grassroots organizations.

Positive Women

I am Prudence Nobantu Mabele. My given name, Nobantu, means "mother of people"; *No* means "mother," and *bantu* means "people." I have been HIV-positive for fourteen years, and I am one of the fortunate people living with HIV today because every day I have a nutritious meal, shelter, clean water, and sanitation. I work out at the gym, take vitamins, practice safer sex, and get lots of support from friends and family. Because of my positive attitude, I have learned a lot about this disease.

I am the founder and executive director of the Positive Women's Network. I enjoy working with women who are HIV-positive; I help them to accept their status and then encourage them to do many good things with their lives — because they will not die now. Life can be good in spite of this sickness. When you have a job or are doing something, you will always be happy, as you can be self-reliant and take good care of yourself. At the Positive Women's Network we teach women to create artwork; they do bead work and make earrings and many other things so that they can earn a salary, which will help them raise their children and give them a brighter future. We also encourage people to go back to school, and we help them with subjects that are useful and will make them marketable in their future careers.

What I like about our time in history is that there are opportunities. We can go to universities and schools, and at the same time we can preserve our cultural and spiritual heritage. I want to thank the people who fought for our rights in South Africa. Now we have opportunities like jobs and schools that are free for all. People of our nation today, both black and white, are treated as equals, and we have good race relations. There are problems, but they can be solved, and I believe they *will* be solved.

What defines my generation are the young women of diverse backgrounds who have a bit of everything — like culture, religion, an outgoing attitude, education, and spirituality. I define myself as one of these women, and HIV/AIDS will not stop me from achieving my goals and inspiring others to reach theirs.

[FROM THE ORIGINAL XHOSA]

Okunika inkcazelo ngexesha endiphila kulo ngabasetyhini abaselula nabamvelaphi yahlukahlukeneyo benolwazi olungephi ngento yonke - njengenkcubeko, inkolo, uluvo lokuzikhupha, imfundo nokukholwa kwiminyanya. Ndizichaza njengomnye wabasetyhini abanjalo, yaye ugawulayo nentsholongwane yakhe abasayi kundithintela ekufezekiseni iinjongo zam nokuphembelela abanye ukuba bafezekise ezabo.

NURUL IZZAH ANWAR • MALAYSIA

Nurul Izzah Anwar, born in Malaysia in 1980, is the daughter of former Deputy Prime Minister of Malaysia Anwar Ibrahim. The imprisonment in 1998 of her father, protested by human rights groups worldwide, served as a catalyzing force for her involvement with the Reformasi Movement. This group encourages democracy in Malaysia through economic and political reform. Anwar Ibrahim was released in September 2004, just before Nurul graduated from college with a degree in electronics and electrical engineering.

The Mechanics of My Hope

Regrets, they say, are a part of life. A life led without regrets is a life not well lived. I've had regrets, as I'm sure most of us have. I am not regretful of how my life has turned out, but instead, I am regretful of how slow I was in becoming committed to my ideals, in joining the movement to create a better world.

Life for me began with a certain sense of normalcy. It was definitely devoid of any feeling of youthful idealism until September 1998, when my father was wrongfully imprisoned.

August of that year saw me as a young teenager without a strong sense of conviction or idealism. They say ignorance is bliss; perhaps that categorically explains much of what I was feeling at that particular time — a time of busy studying and hanging out with friends, unconscious of worldly cares. That month, I wrote a letter to my dear father. It was his birthday present, since there was little choice of material presents in the dusty town of Tronoh, where I was studying. I wrote it while I was ignoring my lectures and missing my family, especially my father.

I knew little of my father's student activism back on campus, except for the things that my uncles and aunts would tell me. Father would often joke about his cabinet experiences — or rather, mishaps — about his leadership at the University Malaya, the famous demonstrations that we kids know so little about. His earlier incarceration in 1974 was never discussed thoroughly with the rest of us. I wondered how he overcame that particular challenge.

In my letter, I asked him to tell me about all of these experiences, and I eagerly awaited a response. But, as God had planned it, September 1998 arrived the next month. Before I knew it, ironically, we were living the answers to the questions I asked.

Everything happened at once. The world, filled with such innocence and lighthearted candor before, slowly became blurred with uncertainty and apprehension. It was a period of pure darkness and fright, when our only solace came from our belief in God, and the phrase that was constantly repeated was that whatever happens, whatever anyone does to us, God will somehow save us.

A small flicker of hope appeared about a week after my father's detention. Destiny had it that I should travel abroad — to further the cause for reform in my country, to advance the call for justice, and to reach out to the outside world for their support for our efforts to promote democratic reform in Malaysia. It proved to be one of the most difficult and formidable tasks that I have ever had to perform.

Challenges and choices present themselves in a most peculiar way. I had to decide whether I would meet with the presidents of Indonesia and the Philippines to ask for their help. I was eighteen years of age, clueless about world politics, and extremely discouraged.

But there is beauty in being naïve because you never lose sight of hope — hope for a better

continued

tomorrow, or in the Asian context, hope for a more constructive diplomacy. I caught a glimmer of that hope as I shook hands with President Habibie of Indonesia and President Estrada of the Philippines. I remember the risk these leaders took and the kindness they granted to me, the daughter of a prisoner who was wrongfully accused. Yes, maybe it was natural for me to champion my father's cause, for I am his daughter. But for them, and for the hundreds of thousands of people who have thrown caution to the wind to support our movement for democracy and reform? How did they find the courage to take such risks?

Then, stopping myself, I started to remember the many political prisoners through history who have spent each restless night in an empty, dark, and lonely cell. How on earth did they cope with the bleakness of reality? These people had suffered greatly, but their souls remained strong, their convictions harder than steel.

And slowly, it came to me. I could no longer hide in my cocoon of safety and not knowing. I had to embrace the challenge of being a voice for change, and accept it as the will of God. For, according to the Koran, "On no soul does Allah place a burden greater than he can bear" (Al-Baqarah, verse 286), and there exists *hikmah* (wisdom) in every experience that graces our life.

As I write this, it has been three years since the imprisonment took place. The reform movement in Malaysia has taken on a quieter tone, with repression of speech, the total government control of mainstream media, and the jailing of opposition leaders. The September 11 terrorist attacks in the United States have led to an increased crackdown on opposition. But all this should not be a seen as a despondent time in the struggle. My heart quaked in fear every time my father made reference to the laboriously long struggle of Nelson Mandela, who spent twenty-seven years in jail before apartheid was successfully abolished. But yet, it did provide a sense of solace and a glimmer of hope for the future. The three years we have spent fighting for reform is not a long time, judging by the normal standards of a struggle, and we will certainly pass through many trials and tribulations before we succeed. "And fight them on, until there is no more tumult or oppression, and there prevail justice and faith in Allah" (Al-Baqarah, verse 193). "And do thou be patient, for thy patience is but from Allah; nor grieve over them, and distress not thyself because of their plots. For Allah is

with those who restrain themselves and those who do good" (An-Nahl, verses 127–28).

In living through these dark moments, I have found my answers — the answers to the questions I asked my father, and my own answers for life. These experiences have shaped me into who I am now. In some ways, I am not different from the young, impressionable teenage girl I was before. In other ways, everything — from how I greet each coming day to how meaningful a fatherly hug can be — has changed forever.

We will all encounter questions in this life — simple questions dealing with the mundane to philosophical questions dealing with the meaning of our existence. The important thing is to remember to reach out for the answers, to try with all our might to fulfill our mission to reinvigorate humanity. Never take happiness, love, justice, and all things virtuous for granted. Hold them dearly within your heart, for in all of these virtues lie the essence of God.

And to all this, and so much more, I have one main person to thank and to cherish for the rest of my life — my beloved father, Anwar Ibrahim.

3

BETWEEN

BEING PART OF TWO OR MORE **WORLDS.** FEELING NOT QUITE **AT HOME** IN EITHER. BEING **PRESSURED** TO CHOOSE BETWEEN THEM. DECIDING TO CREATE **YOUR OWN.**

As we went through young women's responses to our call for submissions, the sentiment of straddling two or more worlds kept repeating itself, drawing a common thread between women in the most diverse of settings and circumstances.

In Macedonia, Enisa Eminova sits quarreling with her grandmother. A young Roma (gypsy) woman, Enisa has taken advantage of the new opportunities available to her generation. She has moved to the country's capital and studied at a university, and she now has a job in the international nonprofit sector. But her grandmother thinks she is becoming too Westernized and is especially upset at the idea of Enisa dating. Enisa feels forced to choose between her career and her family's traditions. She wants to find a way to balance the two.

In South Africa, Erika Hibbert reflects on her experience coming of age in a country that is trying to come to terms with its past. A white South African, she recalls going to the beach as child and being told that there were no black people there because "blacks don't like water." Today she and other young women struggle to heal the wounds of their country's divisive history. They can't change the color of their skin, but they strive to create a world in which color does not determine anyone's destiny.

In a college town in the United States, someone asks Elda Stanco where she is from. Born and raised in Venezuela, having worked in Spain, holding an Italian passport, and educated in North America, Elda takes a deep breath, wondering if she should indeed share the thirty-minute transatlantic saga of her upbringing. She thinks about all the friends she has who have their own stories of mixed heritage and multiple immigrations. She wonders: Isn't it about time to stop classifying young women by their nationalities?

• • •

Motion. Movement.

Webster's online dictionary defines the word *between* as a word "used in expressing motion from one body or place to another." In our lifetimes, we have witnessed a dramatic acceleration of movement of people, goods, and even ideas between and within nations. In recent decades, the amount of money spent on global tourism has skyrocketed. As of July 2005, the Internet had found a place in the lives of more than 900 million people worldwide, making it the fastest-spreading communications technology in history.[1] International trade in goods and services between countries continues to explode. This dramatic movement between cultures and nations defines the experiences of many young women today.

We begin part 3 with a section called "Generations." In this era of rapid globalization, how do today's young women relate to the very different experiences and perspectives of their mothers and grandmothers? By and large, they do so with great admiration and respect. Katerina Otcenaskova-Richtr, from the Czech Republic, became an artist while everyone else in her family remained part of the working class. She took full advantage of the career opportunities in the art world available to her generation, but she made a point of acknowledging that her mother's love and support made this goal achievable for her. Likewise, Australian Nina Cullen's beautiful essay, "Mother Tongue," pays tribute to her German immigrant mother, reflecting on the differences in their values but concluding with how much she admires her mother's example. "If I'm a quarter of the woman she is," Nina writes, "I'm a lucky girl."

The second section is called "Borders & Identity." It includes the experiences of immigrants and the daughters of mixed marriage and the voices of those who travel out of necessity (such as Laura Boushnak, a Palestinian refugee) and those who travel because they want to (like Giada Ripa di Meana, an Italian artist who has lived and worked on three continents).

While the mixing of identities can be a source of confusion, it can also be a source of great opportunity. For example, Pireeni Sundaralingam, a refugee from Sri Lanka's civil war who now lives in the United States, uses her access to Western audiences to write poetry that reminds people that violent conflict is everyone's problem. And Rebecca Walker, a young American writer who is half Jewish and half black, reflects on her mixed upbringing in order to encourage readers to move beyond stereotypes about racial and ethnic identity.

We are taking advantage of increasingly blurred boundaries — between nations, between ethnic groups, between urban and rural, and between women and men — to create new opportunities and new pathways in life. We are connecting more and more with each other across these boundaries, and we are handling this challenge with exuberance, humor, and strength. In so doing, we are ensuring that our generation of women emerges as a powerful creative force in the twenty-first century.

FACTS & TRENDS

>> Since 1950, world trade in goods has increased by twenty-six times.[2]

>> The gender gap in Internet use is quickly disappearing. In Thailand, for example, women comprised 35 percent of users in 1999, compared with 49 percent in 2000. In the United States, in 1996 38 percent of users were women; in 2000 51 percent were. In Brazil, Internet use has spiked in recent years, and women make up 47 percent of users there.[3]

>> A total of 175 million people (3 percent of the world's population) resided outside of their country of birth as of 2001, and 20 million of these people were refugees.[4] In 1982, there were an estimated 1.2 million internally displaced persons (IDPs) in eleven countries; two decades later, as a result of armed conflict, there are as many as twenty-five million IDPs in more than forty nation-states.[5] Women and children constitute some 80 percent of refugees and other displaced persons, including IDPs.[6]

>> Eighty percent of all travel decisions in the United States are made by women.[7] As of 2005, women constituted 48 percent of business travelers in the United States.[8]

>> In the coming years, the growth of the middle class in Asia will produce a significant increase of women travelers from Japan, Hong Kong, Singapore, South Korea, and Taiwan.[9]

>> Between 1987 and 1996, the number of women travelers from Hong Kong increased over 120 percent, from 2.11 million to 4.7 million.[10]

GENERATIONS

MARGARITA MARIA SERRANO-MORENO • COLOMBIA

Margarita Maria Serrano-Moreno was born in 1977 in Cali, Colombia, and she now lives in Madison, Wisconsin. After finishing her bachelor of arts in Bogotá, Margarita decided to travel to the United States in an attempt to understand more of herself and her culture by being in a different one. Gender in her own culture has been one of her main themes; she portrays the women of her family as representatives of the Colombian culture.

LEFT *Timeless Displacement*

I began photographing sixteen-year-old girls in New Delhi in November 2002 for a documentary project entitled *Sweet Sixteen.* For the exhibit, I used personal narratives of the girls alongside their images.

The testimonials written by these girls were a revelation to me. I'm thirty years old — almost twice the age of the girls I'm photographing. For me, their writings revealed an enormous generation gap, much more than the gap I felt with my mother's generation. My teen years were idyllic, much calmer in contrast. I used to ride my bicycle, play table tennis, and spend a lot of time reading. Cable TV didn't exist. The highlight of the week was the Sunday movie on national TV, which kept my mother glued to the screen, while I snuck away to meet my boyfriend. Conversations about sex were taboo when I was a teen.

Sixteen is such a formative year in a young woman's life. Girls today are becoming women far ahead of their time. Peer pressure is extraordinary. The self-image is constantly changing. For many, sixteen is a very narcissistic age — the birth of self-awareness is always much more complex in the head. Beauty pageants in India today have found national sanction and glory. Indian cinema is a perfect barometer of the changing values in society. Role models for the young Indian teen are therefore bound to change.

Modernity and tradition have never been at such a crossroads, and I do believe that this generation is on the cusp of a culture clash between Eastern and Western values. Female roles are being renegotiated and redefined. Adolescent angst is a universal phenomenon, which is a precious indicator of the past and the apprehensions about the future.

Sweet Sixteen is essentially about that in-between stage between girlhood and womanhood. It is about contradictory minds, the birth of female aspirations, and identity in modern India.

ANITA KHEMKA • INDIA

Anita Khemka is an Indian photographer in her thirties. Her previous photographic journals dealt with sexuality as the main theme. She is interested in the changing roles of women in her culture and in teenage girls' perceptions of themselves and their external environments.

RIGHT AND FOLLOWING PAGES *Sweet Sixteen* series

Our Family Tribe

I work as a training assistant at a Member Practice of Ernst & Young Global, slaving for a monthly salary that will enable me to buy the groceries for my family, enroll in a foreign language course, pursue a master's degree in media studies, and earn enough to take a vacation out of this country within two years — hopefully for good.

In my last name, Dugeña, the g is pronounced as an h, so it is pronounced as "doo-hen-ya." It is Spanish-sounding — probably because it is European in origin; my father was born in Cebu, the first Philippine island that the European explorer Ferdinand Magellan set foot on. Sometimes, some people who try to pronounce my last name do so with a question mark sound at the end, as if seeking to confirm that they got it right; most don't. Dugena, minus the tilde, also happens to be the brand name of a German-made watch. Unfortunately, we are not in any way related to the manufacturers. My middle name is Jornales, pronounced "hor-na-less"; the j is pronounced as an h. With all the silent letters and pronunciation complexities in my name, an office-mate once wondered why I am called Jenny instead of Henny.

I live in a tightly knit Catholic family with middle-class sentiments and morality. My immediate family (composed of my mother, my father, and my younger sister), my aunt's family (her husband, her son, her daughter, her daughter's son, and the man cohabiting with her daughter), and my grandparents on my mother's side all live together on a one-hundred-square-meter lot in a congested part of Pasay City. My grandparents bought the lot decades ago from its previous owner, whom my grandmother worked for as a maid. The house and the whole lot are among the, if not the only, prized possessions of my grandparents. Owing to the emotion and history attached to their home, my grandparents refuse to sell it or move to a cleaner, less crime-prone area. I have never fully understood their reasoning, so I think otherwise — especially when a quarrel, a fist fight, or a scream is heard nightly from our neighbors.

My immediate family's house is under my grandparents' house; our ceiling is their bedroom floor. My aunt's house is beside ours — literally beside it; their wall is our wall, and their ceiling is my grandparents' living room floor. So it is not unusual for us to know about all of the events, or nonevents, in each other's lives without anyone telling any vivid stories. We see, hear, and feel everything.

As a child, this setup served me well. I didn't mind being barged in on while lip-synching a song on TV or playacting a character; I was oblivious to anyone's opinion. As I grew up, however, I was influenced by programs on TV where each individual had a room of his or her own, and I wondered, why don't I? I grew conscious of the fact that we live together the way we do. After that, I did mind being barged in on, be it by my cousins, grandmother, or aunts. I found it intolerable to live constantly "on

JENNIFER JORNALES DUGEÑA • PHILIPPINES

Jennifer Jornales Dugeña was born and raised in the Philippines and lives in Pasay City, south of Manila, with her family.

my toes" lest someone see my solitary activities in all their forms. When I had a boyfriend, I realized the futility of my need for privacy. But I also appreciate the connectedness we have in my family, the way we are easily at the beck and call of the other family members living on one lot with many roofs.

In our family tribe, everyone believes that harmony is achieved by not rocking the boat. Family confrontations, even with the best intentions, mean dissent. It is better to suffer in silence than to speak one's mind and challenge the existing familial condition. If you must speak, you should do so in symbols — and you must address the wind or a person unrelated to the topic at hand in the hope that the air may carry it away from our house and send it towards the appropriate addressee.

Now I know why I hate confrontations. I either suffer in silence or avoid a person or event altogether — unless the confrontation is to defend a family member. Only then do I budge. If the confrontation is for my own cause, I would rather brush it off and try to not be bothered by it. If ever I do confront a person or situation, it is always in jest. Sometimes I hate myself for this. Most of the time, I hate that my family bred into us such a psychological condition. If only my family members were not stuck on their own concepts of themselves and did not live by others' standards! They shouldn't value other people's opinions so much or compare their lives and selves with others. I cannot help but feel the need for change. Instead of things getting better, it seems that time has stopped — it is stuck. All of my family members seem afraid of change. I don't want to be afraid of it any longer. I want change.

To uncondition what has been programmed in me is my personal quest. I think I need a personal space to grow into my own self — with all the familiar genealogical strings of passivity, mediocrity, and insecurity detached from me, to do what I need to do in spite of their judgments or opinion. So help me, God.

ENISA EMINOVA • MACEDONIA

Enisa Eminova was born in 1982 in a small, rural Roma (gypsy) community in Macedonia, where her father owns horses and donkeys. As one of very few Roma college students in her country, Enisa studied economics at Sts. Cyril and Methodius University in Skopje, Macedonia. In 2001 she helped organize a campaign against using public virginity tests on Roma women before marriage. Enisa now manages the Roma Women's Initiative for the Open Society Institute.

Choosing between Two Paths

[Parts of this essay are excerpted from "On Virginity — Vas o chaipen"]

I am a Roma (gypsy) girl from Eastern Europe, and I must choose between two paths. One leads me towards traditions that I must respect because of others' opinions or for the sake of my parents' reputation. That path grabs me and gives me no space to move, but I must follow it simply because I was born a Roma girl. I do not have the right to choose the other direction that gives me the room to sit down, to reflect, to know that I am an individual with my own sense of self, the one who knows how to steer my own life. I am afraid that I might lose my parents if I do.

So I shall live my whole life between the two paths, practicing the one called tradition. I shall never be a person who can say, "I have an idea. I know how to solve the problem." That will always be done by someone else, and I shall stand aside, watching someone else deciding for me, someone who is unwilling to hear that I already know what I want.

Just because I decided to study, to get a better job, to be integrated into society, and to choose my partner, I will be labeled as a *Gadzi* (non-Roma) or as a crazy Roma. The only important criterion for those who decide whether I am smart, whether I come from a good family, whether I should be respected, and so on, is my virginity! I must remain a virgin until marriage just because this gives my family a better reputation — otherwise they will disown me or will be disappointed to death.

Once I asked my grandmother, "Grandma, how old were you when you got married?"

She responded, "Well, I was fifteen, I think." (She is seventy-five now.)

And I asked, "Does this mean that you had sex when you were fifteen?"

She said, "How come you dare to ask such a question?" She was very put out, but she finally said, "Yes, I had sex when I was fifteen. What does this have to do with you?"

So I tried to summarize, saying, "Well, you had no education and no job, you were fifteen, and you decided to get married. I am twenty-one, going to university, speaking English, et cetera, and still I must remain a virgin? Just because I decided to study instead of getting married?"

Then she got even madder and said something like, "Oh, my God! Are you trying to say you are not a virgin anymore?! Listen, if you want to have sex, then get married!"

When I asked her why my virginity is important to her or how she benefits from the situation, she said, "Enough!" Then she went to my house to tell my mother everything I had said and to say she thinks I am not a virgin anymore. Of course, then I had to go through some arguments with my family to explain that I am the only one who creates my own life and future. The outcome of this mess is that:

1. my family thinks that I am becoming *Gadzi* (non-Roma);
2. they think I am crazy;
3. they regret allowing me to join the nonprofit sector, where I travel a lot, have non-Roma friends, and so on;
4. they are trying to understand me, but my logic is foreign to them so they are slowly giving up.

So, this is my overview. If the Roma girls in my country want to "stay" Roma, most of them must choose either following their own needs and fulfilling their own expectations or following other people's expectations — their parents', the community's, and so on. It is so difficult to balance!

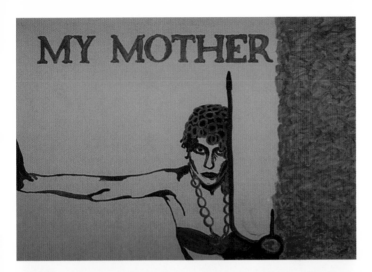

I am the only artist in our family. The others belong to the "working classes." However, my grandmother is the one closest to my heart. She is "the lady from the capital," the lady from Prague. The lives of people in Prague have always been different from those of people who live in a small town. My grandmother is the extravagant woman of my family, and her big-city roots are evident in the way she dresses and communicates with her surroundings. In the village, people have to accept her just the way she is. I have always been fascinated by her hats, caps, shoes, and color combinations; I always wanted to be like my grandmother from the big city.

My mother and her sewing machine made my wish possible. She knew what I wanted and supported me. Now she is proud of me. I'm the well-known artist, you know? My mother achieved through me something she otherwise never could reach. She had to be the woman who looks after her children, who takes care of her husband and home — a housewife. The world of a small town held my mother in a firm grip. I ran away, escaped.

I am an artist. I am strange. Wait — am I strange? No, nowadays a daughter working as an artist is a normal thing.

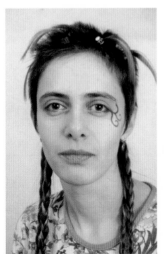

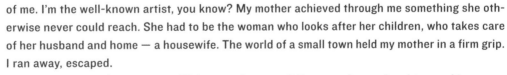

KATERINA OTCENASKOVA-RICHTR • CZECH REPUBLIC

Katerina Otcenaskova-Richtr was born in 1974 in the Czech Republic. In March 2005 she lost her battle with cancer and passed away. She lived near the sea in Sweden with her family, and she is survived by her husband, Jaroslav Richtr. Katerina received a formal education in art and Czech literature at J. E. Purkyně University. She used mixed-media projects to experiment with her relationships to her own body, women's identity, sexuality, fashion, and family.

ABOVE *My Mother* and *My Sister*

Olga Vladimirskaya (above): I think the women of my generation are too concerned with being "women." They wear high heels and uncomfortable clothes. By their thirties or forties, many of them feel disappointed because their youth and beauty have passed. Of course, this does not apply to all women. The information agency where I work has produced a special program titled "Women in Business." The businesswomen that we interviewed were happy and optimistic. Rather than blaming men, they spoke of harmonious and fruitful business relations with them. They also spoke about their happy families. I think that my generation has already come to terms with the necessity of becoming "new women," but many do not have the desire or the strength to do it. That's why my hopes are with the younger generation of women, with my daughter and those like her. I am proud that they gladly accept me into their circle. That means I too belong to the generation of "new women" and that our common traits transcend age.

Aleksandra Kovaleva (left): In my opinion, there are many, many factors that define my generation. But I can say one thing: Girls my age have many opportunities and are taking advantage of them all. The doors are open. You can find your own way and stick with it. There's no need to seek out problems; they'll find you sure enough and make you stumble, make you think, "Perhaps I should stop, perhaps I should turn back?" Girls my age don't reflect too much; they simply go forward without looking back. We are confident in ourselves and our strength.

OLGA VLADIMIRSKAYA and ALEKSANDRA KOVALEVA • UKRAINE

Olga Vladimirskaya and Aleksandra Kovaleva, a mother-and-daughter team, have worked with the concept of unity, linking poetry that Olga wrote before Aleksandra was born with Aleksandra's drawings. In this way they celebrate their shared identities as artists and women, despite their differences in age. Aleksandra would like to become a theater director, and Olga works as an editor.

RIGHT *Two Wings*

Wings

[FROM THE ORIGINAL RUSSIAN]

The sky stabbed through the breaches in the ceiling
But we, like silent pilgrims in a shrine,
Exhaled instead of praying. The divine
presence of freedom overwhelmed our feelings.
To roam strange lands, or plunge into the abyss,
Or let your reason burn in passion's blaze . . .
Yet eagles cast their everlasting gaze
from up above, where air is thin like bliss!
A mountain white that wears a snowy crown,
things redolent of life, so packed with lies,
the truth that peers so hard into your eyes
and air so vast the stars are tumbling down.

Крыла

Хоть за кордон, хоть вместе со скалы,
Хоть разум выжги жаром новой страсти,–
Но там, где воздух разрежен, как счастье,
Так пристально с небес глядят орлы!
Так белоснежна горная гряда.
Так несерьезно все, что пахнет жизнью.
Так неотступно в очи смотрит истина.
Так много воздуха, что падает звезда.
Там небо – сквозь проломленные своды.
Но мы молчали, словно это храм.
Мы не молились – мы дышали там,
И с нами бог, спаситель наш – Свобода!

Mother Tongue

Sometimes I think my mum looks at me and thinks she hasn't taught me anything. She shakes her head with the disappointment of a giver of unheeded advice, quietly reminding herself that it's a different world today.

For laughs, I tell my people Mum's maiden name: Lautenschlager — a German in Australia!

When the rest of the world was staging radical change and a new cultural order, my mum was going through her own private revolution. At thirty-eight she took herself off the shelf and caught a plane to Australia. After years of letters, a few photos, a visit, and a proposal, she married my dad, whom she had met in Africa five years earlier.

I do believe in love

I do believe in sex before marriage

I don't assume that I will have one partner all my life

She arrived in Australia in 1974, a farmer's daughter from Bavaria. She didn't know what to think. Her new home was a one-story house with a square of yellow grass out back and a rotating clothesline. Cheese was cheddar, coffee was instant, and cakes were sponge. This was Australia. She was saved from being called a Nazi because she was part of a whole postwar generation of migrants who moved to Australia. She still got funny looks sometimes.

I do believe in taking chances

I do believe in second chances

The graveyards had weeds so high you couldn't read the inscriptions. It was a disgrace. The memory of neat parish plots in her hometown made her sad. It still disappoints her that my uncle doesn't have a tombstone twenty years after his death.

I don't darn

I don't keep ripped stockings

I don't own a glory-box

My mum and her brothers were spared from the Hitler Youth because their dad said they had too far to walk home from the meetings. In big regimes you forget the little people and their own quiet disagreement.

I don't believe in wasting another generation on war

I don't believe the rhetoric that justifies it

My mum wanted to be a chicken woman. They rode motorbikes and told dirty jokes. They worked for the agricultural bureau and were sent out to farms to teach them about chickens. My mum rode her first motorbike when she was fifteen. She was still dressed in black for the mourning of her mother's death.

I do believe in independence

I do believe in strong women

My grandfather made my mum call her stepmother Mamma. It was only a year after her mother had died. With the melancholy of a fifteen-year-old girl grieving, she tried not to address her stepmother at all.

I want to kiss better

NINA CULLEN · AUSTRALIA

Nina Cullen was born in Sydney to an Australian father and a German mother. Her writing reflects an interest in the beauty of all that is domestic and the stories that sit in our own backyards. She has traveled extensively and has worked as a journalist, a teacher, and everything in between in order to keep the words flowing. She has just finished her first novel.

During Holy Week, in a hospital that faced the ocean but a room that faced the town, my mum had her first child. She was classified as an elderly primate, a forty-year-old first-time mother. My dad, a nervous doctor, paced the corridor with anxiety but wasn't allowed in.

I do want children
I do believe in family
I do want to breastfeed

My mum sang lullabies to us in German, rocking us gently to the tunes of her childhood. She bounced over vowels and pronunciation that will never seem natural to me. Now I sing words I'm not sure of to a tune that is forever soothing.

I don't want regret
I don't want loneliness

We celebrate Christmas on Christmas Eve, out of sync with Australian custom. And I was the child who told everyone else Santa didn't exist. I didn't know how to say "hand towel" in English until I was ten years old. I asked for a *Waschlappen* before a bath at my friend's house.

I do believe in holding on to a sense of culture

I learned I was sharing my mum when I was still in high school. I went with her on a client visit. She talked to an old lady, holding her hand, and it was obviously the best part of the lady's week. She was a mother, a friend, a caregiver, a worker, a wife, and a neighbor. This was news to me.

I do believe in a sense of social responsibility

My mum is known for her cooking. Her apple cake is always first to sell at local cake stalls, and her potato salad disappears instantly at family gatherings.

I don't believe a clean house is that important
I don't make chicken stock from bones
I do make a great apple cake and potato salad

My mum is shrinking, slowly, two centimeters so far. She's a little woman who still wields the power to make things better — not all okay, but more okay.

I want to learn from my own mistakes

When we found out my dad was dying, my mum told me that she had a dream where they were in a forest. More religious than superstitious, she said she lost him and was on her own in the darkness. I think sometimes dreams are just dreams, but not always.

I want to grow old holding someone's hand
I do believe in some idea of God

I wonder, does she ever think it's strange that she's standing in a supermarket queue in Sydney, this woman who once got bitten on the stomach by an angry goose as she led the gaggle to water? In her memory, does she mark the time when she strayed from bucolic to suburban?

If I am a quarter of the woman she is, I'm a lucky girl

BORDERS & IDENTITY

ELIANE CRISTINA TESTA • BRAZIL

Eliane Cristina Testa, a painter, poet, and college professor, was born in 1972 in Paraná, Brazil. She developed an aptitude for art at a young age, and she has dedicated her life to the study of literature.

LEFT *Espelhos Étnicos (Ethnic Mirrors)*

As a South Asian Canadian woman of Muslim heritage, my life comprises many intersections and many identities, which are constantly negotiated and renegotiated. Living in this global world, more and more people are caught in the web of global intersections. The seemingly warm notion of a global village is in fact very complex and destabilizing. What does it mean to be from a particular culture? What is culture? How do we begin to define ourselves or understand ourselves in this context of globalization? These are the types of questions that my art investigates.

My art is at once a personal, public, and political exploration. As a second-generation Canadian and a woman of color, I am constantly coming to terms with ideas of dislocation, of being "away from home." However, these feelings of dislocation and isolation and the questioning of identity occur in many people in this global age. My work examines the ephemeral quality of culture and the dynamic flux of identity.

FARHEEN HAQ · CANADA

Farheen Haq, born in 1977, has always been an explorer and is fascinated with communication, language, and symbolism. She was born to a Pakistani family in southern Ontario, Canada. She studied in Toronto, worked in Southeast Asia, and currently resides on Vancouver Island, British Columbia. Her work deals with constructs of identity and cultural inscriptions of the body, especially the female body, and it aims to question these constructs and open up possibilities for dialogue.

ABOVE *They're There Now* RIGHT *Body of Questions*

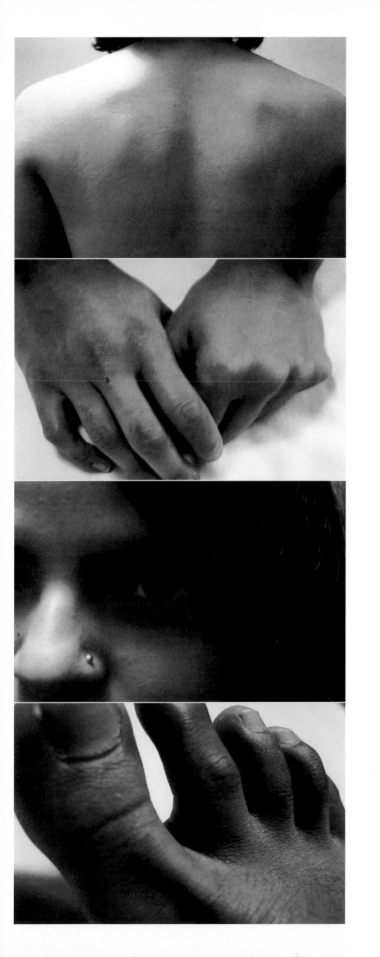

Describe your previous work history.

What is your present occupation?

Marital status:

Any distinguishing features?

The Miseducation of Irie Jones
[An Excerpt from *White Teeth*]

It was dark in Roshi's and smelled strongly of the same scents as PK's: ammonia and coconut oil, pain mixed with pleasure. From the dim glow given off by a flickering strip light, Irie could see there were no shelves to speak of but instead hair products piled like mountains from the floor up, while accessories (combs, bands, nail varnish) were stapled to the walls with the price written in felt-tip alongside. The only display of any recognizable kind was placed just below the ceiling in a loop around the room, taking pride of place like a collection of sacrificial scalps or hunting trophies. Hair. Long tresses stapled a few inches apart. Underneath each a large cardboard sign explaining its pedigree:

2 Meters. Natural Thai. Straight. Chestnut.
1 Meter. Natural Pakistani. Staight with a wave. Black.
5 Meters. Natural Chinese. Straight. Black.
3 Meters. Synthetic hair. Corkscrew curl. Pink.

Irie approached the counter. A hugely fat woman in a sari was waddling to the cash till and back again to hand over twenty-five pounds to an Indian girl whose hair had been shorn haphazardly close to the scalp.

"And please don't be looking at me in that manner. Twenty-five is very reasonable price. I tell you I can't do any more with all these split ends."

The girl objected in another language, picked up the bag of hair in question from the counter, and made as if to leave with it, but the elder woman snatched it away.

"Please, don't embarrass yourself further. We both have seen the ends. Twenty-five is all I can give you for it. You won't get more some other place. Please now," she said, looking over the girl's shoulder to Irie, "other customers I have."

Irie saw hot tears, not unlike her own, spring to the girl's eyes. She seemed to freeze for a moment, vibrating ever so slightly with anger; then she slammed her hand down on the counter, swept up her twenty-five pounds and headed for the door.

The fat lady shook her chins in contempt after the disappearing girl. "Ungrateful, she is."

Then she unpeeled a sticky label from its brown-paper backing and slapped it on the bag of hair. It said: "6 Meters. Indian. Straight. Black/red."

"Yes, dear. What is it I can do?"

ZADIE SMITH • UNITED KINGDOM

Zadie Smith was born in northwest London in 1975 and continues to live in the area. Her first novel, *White Teeth*, was the winner of the Whitbread First Novel Award, *The Guardian* First Book Award, the James Tait Black Memorial Prize for Fiction, and the Commonwealth Writers' First Book Award. Her second novel, *The Autograph Man*, won *The Jewish Quarterly* Wingate Literary Prize and was long-listed for the Man Booker Prize. Her third novel, *On Beauty*, was published in September 2005, and she is working on a book of essays on ethical thought in twentieth-century fiction. She is a Fellow of the Royal Society of Literature.

Irie repeated Andrea's instruction and handed over the card.

"Eight packets? That is about six meters, no?"

"I don't know."

"Yes, yes, it is. You want it straight or with a wave?"

"Straight. Dead straight."

The fat lady did a silent calculation and then picked up the bag of hair that the girl had just left. "This is what you're looking for. I haven't been able to package it, you understand. But it is absolutely clean. You want?"

Irie looked dubious.

"Don't worry about what I said. No split ends. Just silly girl trying to get more than she deserves. Some people got no understanding of simple economics . . . It hurts her to cut off her hair, so a million pounds she expects or something crazy. Beautiful hair, she has. When I was young, oh, mine was beautiful too, eh?" The fat lady erupted into high-pitched laughter, her busy upper lip making her mustache quiver. The laugh subsided.

"Tell Andrea that will be thirty-seven fifty. We Indian women have the beautiful hair, hey? Everybody wants it!"

A black woman with children in a twin buggy was waiting behind Irie with a packet of hairpins. She sucked her teeth. "You people think you're all Mr. Bigstuff," she muttered, half to herself.

"Some of us are happy with our African hair, thank you very much. I don't want to buy some poor Indian girl's hair. And I wish to God I could buy black hair products from black people for once. How we going to make it in this country if we don't make our own business?"

The skin around the fat lady's mouth became very tight. She began talking twelve to the dozen, putting Irie's hair in a bag and writing her out a receipt, addressing all her comments to the woman's interjections. "You don't like shopping here, then please don't be shopping here — is forcing you anybody? No, is anybody? It's amazing: people, the rudeness, I am not a racist, but I can't understand it, I'm just providing a service, a service. I don't need abuse, just leave your money on the counter, if I am getting abuse, I'm not serving."

"No one's givin' you abuse. Jesus Christ!"

"Is it my fault if they want the hair that is straight — and paler skin sometimes, like Michael Jackson, my fault he is too? They tell me not to sell the Dr. Peacock Whitener — local paper, my God,

continued

what a fuss! — and then they buy it — take that receipt to Andrea, will you, my dear, please? I'm just trying to make a living in this country like the rest of everybody. There you are, dear, there's your hair."

The woman reached around Irie and delivered the right change to the counter with an angry smash. "For fuck's sake!"

"I can't help it if that's what they want — supply, demand. And bad language, I won't tolerate! Simple economics — mind your step on the way out, dear — and *you*, no, don't come back, please, I will call the police, I won't be threatened, the police, I will call them."

"Yeah, yeah, *yeah*."

Irie held the door open for the double buggy, and took one side to help carry it over the front step. Outside the woman put her hairpins in her pocket. She looked exhausted.

"I hate that place," she said. "But I need hairpins."

"I need hair," said Irie.

The woman shook her head. "You've *got* hair," she said.

Five and a half hours later, thanks to an arduous operation that involved attaching somebody else's hair in small sections to Irie's own two inches and sealing it with glue, Irie Jones had a full head of long, straight, reddish-black hair.

"Is it straight?" she asked, disbelieving the evidence of her own eyes.

"Straight as hell," said Andrea, admiring her handiwork. "But honey, you're going to have to braid it properly if you want it to stay in. Why won't you let me do it? It won't stay in if it's loose like that."

"It will," said Irie, bewitched by her own reflection. "It's got to."

He — Millat — need only see it once, after all, just once. To ensure she reached him in pristine state, she walked all the way to the Iqbal house with her hands on her hair, terrified that the wind would displace it.

Alsana answered the door. "Oh, hello. No, he's not here. Out. Don't ask me where, he doesn't tell me a thing. I know where Magid is more of the time."

Irie walked into the hallway and caught a sneaky glance of herself in the mirror. Still there and all in the right place.

"Can I wait in here?"

"Of course. You look different, dearie. Lost weight?"

Irie glowed. "New haircut."

"Oh yes . . . you look like a newsreader. Very nice. Now in the living room, please. Niece-of-Shame and her nasty friend are in there, but try not to let that bother you. I'm working in the kitchen and Samad is weeding, so keep the noise down."

Irie walked into the living room. "Bloody hell!" screeched Neena at the approaching vision. "What the fuck do you look like!"

She looked beautiful. She looked straight, un-kinky. Beautiful.

"You look like a freak! Fuck me! Maxine, man, check this out. Jesus Christ, Irie. What exactly were you aiming for?"

Wasn't it obvious? Straight. Straightness. Flick-ability.

"I mean, what was the grand plan? The Negro Meryl Streep?" Neena folded over like a duvet and laughed herself silly.

"Niece-of-Shame!" came Alsana's voice from the kitchen. "Sewing requires concentration. Shut it up, Miss Big-Mouth, please!"

Neena's "nasty friend," otherwise known as Neena's girlfriend, a sexy and slender girl called Maxine with a beautiful porcelain face, dark eyes, and a lot of curly brown hair, gave a pull to Irie's peculiar bangs. "What have you done? You had *beautiful hair,* man. All curly and wild. It was gorgeous."

Irie couldn't say anything for a moment. She had not considered the possibility that she looked anything less than terrific.

"I just had a haircut. What's the big deal?"

"But that's not *your* hair, for fuck's sake, that's

some poor oppressed Pakistani woman who needs the cash for her kids," said Neena, giving it a tug and being rewarded with a handful of it. "OH SHIT!"

Neena and Maxine had a hysteria relapse.

"Just get *off* it, OK?" Irie retreated to an armchair and tucked her knees up under her chin. Trying to sound offhand, she asked, "So . . . umm . . . where's Millat?"

"Is that what all this is in aid of?" asked Neena, astonished. "My shit-for-brains cousin-gee?"

"No. Fuck off."

"Well, he's not here. He's got some new bird. Eastern-bloc gymnast with a stomach like a washboard. Not unattractive, spectacular tits, but tight-assed as hell. Name . . . name?"

"Stasia," said Maxine, looking up briefly from *Top of the Pops*. "Or some such bollocks."

Irie sank deeper into the ruined springs of Samad's favorite chair.

"Irie, will you take some advice? Ever since I've known you, you've been following that boy around like a lost dog. And in that time he's snogged everyone, *everyone* apart from you. He's even snogged *me*, and I'm his first cousin, for fuck's sake."

"And me," said Maxine, "and I'm not that way inclined."

"Haven't you ever wondered why he hasn't snogged you?"

"Because I'm ugly. And fat. With an Afro."

"No, fuckface, because you're all he's *got*. He *needs* you. You two have history. You really *know* him. Look how confused he is. One day he's Allah this, Allah that. Next minute it's big busty blondes, Russian gymnasts, and a smoke of the sinsemilla. He doesn't know his arse from his elbow. Just like his father. He doesn't know who he is. But *you* know him, at least a little, you've known all the sides of him. And he needs that. You're different."

Irie rolled her eyes. Sometimes you want to be different. And sometimes you'd give the hair on your head to be the same as everybody else.

"Look: you're a smart cookie, Irie. But you've been taught all kinds of shit. You've got to reeducate yourself. Realize your value, stop the slavish devotion, and get a life, Irie. Get a girl, get a guy, but get a life."

"You're a very sexy girl, Irie," said Maxine sweetly.

"Yeah. Right."

"Trust her, she's a raving dyke," said Neena, ruffling Maxine's hair affectionately and giving her a kiss. "But the truth is the Barbra Streisand cut you've got there ain't doing shit for you. The Afro was cool, man. It was wicked. It was *yours*."

Suddenly Alsana appeared at the doorway with an enormous plate of biscuits and a look of intense suspicion. Maxine blew her a kiss.

"Biscuits, Irie? Come and have some biscuits. With me. In the kitchen."

Neena groaned. "Don't panic, Auntie. We're not enlisting her into the cult of Sappho."

"I don't *care* what you're doing. I don't *know* what you're doing. I don't *want* to know such things."

"We're watching *television*."

It was Madonna on the TV screen, working her hands around two conically shaped breasts.

"Very nice, I'm sure," sniped Alsana, glaring at Maxine. "Biscuits, Irie?"

"*I'd* like some biscuits," murmured Maxine with a flutter of her extravagant eyelashes.

"I am certain," said Alsana slowly and pointedly, translating code, "I don't have the kind *you* like."

Neena and Maxine fell about all over again.

"Irie?" said Alsana, indicating the kitchen with a grimace. Irie followed her out.

"I'm as liberal as the next person," complained Alsana, once they were alone. "But why do they always have to be laughing and making a song-and-dance about everything? I cannot believe homosexuality is that much fun. Heterosexuality certainly is not."

"I don't think I want to hear that word in this house again," said Samad deadpan, stepping in from the garden and laying his weeding gloves on the table.

continued

"Which one?"

"Either. I am trying my level best to run a godly house."

Samad spotted a figure at his kitchen table, frowned, decided it was indeed Irie Jones and began on the little routine the two of then had going. "Hello, Miss Jones. And how is your father?"

Iris shrugged on cue. "You see him more than we do. How's God?"

"Perfectly fine, thank you. Have you seen my good-for-nothing son recently?"

"Not recently."

"What about my good son?"

"Not for years."

"Will you tell the good-for-nothing he's a good-for-nothing when you find him?"

"I'll do my best, Mr. Iqbal."

"God bless you."

"Gesundheit."

"Now, if you will excuse me." Samad reached for his prayer mat from the top of the fridge and left the room.

"What's the matter with *him*?" asked Irie, noticing that Samad had delivered his lines with less than enthusiasm. "He seems, I don't know, *sad.*"

Alsana sighed. "He *is* sad. He feels like he has screwed everything up. Of course, he *has* screwed everything up, but then again, who will cast the first stone, et cetera. He prays and prays. But he will not look straight at the facts: Millat hanging around with God knows what kind of people, always with the white girls, and Magid . . ."

Irie remembered her first sweetheart encircled by a fuzzy halo of perfection, an illusion born of the disappointment Millat had afforded her over the years.

"Why, what's wrong with Magid?"

Alsana frowned and reached up to the top kitchen shelf, where she collected a thin airmail envelope and passed it to Irie. Irie removed the letter and the photograph inside.

The photo was of Magid, now a tall, distinguished-looking young man. His hair was the deep black of his brother's, but it was not brushed forward on his face. It was parted on the left side, slicked down, and drawn behind the right ear. He was dressed in a tweed suit and what looked — though one couldn't be sure, the photo was not good — like a cravat. He held a large sun hat in one hand. In the other he clasped the hand of the eminent Indian writer Sir R. V. Saraswati. Saraswati was dressed all in white, with his broad-brimmed hat on his head and an ostentatious cane in his free hand. The two of them were posed in a somewhat self-congratulatory manner, smiling broadly and looking for all the world as if they were about to pat each other roundly on the back or had just done so. The midday sun was out and bouncing off Dhaka University's front steps, where the whole scene had been captured.

Alsana inched a smear off the photo with her index finger. "You know Saraswati?"

Irie nodded. Compulsory GCSE text: *A Stitch in Time* by R. V. Saraswati. A bittersweet tale of the last days of Empire.

"Samad hates Saraswati, you understand. Calls him colonial-throwback, English licker-of-behinds."

Irie picked a paragraph at random from the letter and read aloud.

As you can see, I was lucky enough to meet India's very finest writer one bright day in March. After winning an essay competition (my title: "Bangladesh — To Whom May She Turn?"), I traveled to Dhaka to collect my prize (a certificate and a small cash reward) from the great man himself in a ceremony at the university. I am honored to say he took a liking to me and we spent a most pleasant afternoon together; a long, intimate tea followed by a stroll through Dhaka's more appealing prospects. During our lengthy conversations Sir Saraswati commended my mind, and even went so far as to say (and I quote) that I was "a first-rate young man" — a comment I shall treasure! He suggested my future might lie in the law, the university, or even his own profession of the creative pen! I told him the first-

mentioned vocation was closest to my heart and that it had long been my intention to make the Asian countries sensible places, where order prevailed, disaster was prepared for, and a young boy was in no danger from a falling vase (!) New laws, new stipulations, are required (I told him) to deal with our unlucky fate, the natural disaster. But then he corrected me: "Not fate," he said. "Too often we Indians, we Bengalis, we Pakistanis, throw up our hands and cry 'Fate!' in the face of history. But many of us are uneducated, many of us do not understand the world. We must be more like the English. The English fight fate to the death. They do not listen to history unless it is telling them what they wish to hear. We say 'It had to be!' It does not have to be. Nothing does." In one afternoon I learned more from this great man than —

"He learns nothing!"

Samad marched back into the kitchen in a fury and threw the kettle on the stove. "He learns nothing from a man who knows nothing! Where is his beard? Where is his khamise? Where is his humility? If Allah says there will be storm, there will be storm. If he says earthquake, it will be earthquake. Of course it has to be! That is the very reason I sent the child there — to understand that essentially we are weak, that we are not in control. What does Islam mean? What does the word, the very word, mean? *I surrender.* I surrender to God. I surrender to him. This is not my life, this is his life. This life I call mine is his to do with what he will. Indeed, I shall be tossed and turned on the wave, and there shall be nothing to be done. Nothing! Nature itself is Muslim, because it obeys the laws the creator has ingrained in it."

"Don't you preach in this house, Samad Miah! There are places for that sort of thing. Go to mosque, but don't do it in the kitchen, people have to be eating in here — "

"But we, we do not automatically obey. We are tricky, we are the tricky bastards, we humans. We have the evil inside us, the free will. We must *learn* to obey. That is what I sent the child Magid Mahfooz Murshed Mubtasim Iqbal to discover. Tell me, did I send him to have his mind poisoned by a Rule-Britannia-worshiping Hindu old queen?"

"Maybe, Samad Miah, maybe not."

"Don't, Alsi, I warn you — "

"Oh, go on, you old pot-boiler!" Alsana gathered her spare tires around her like a sumo wrestler. "You say we have no control, yet you always try to control everything! Let *go*, Samad Miah. Let the boy go. He is second generation — he was born here — naturally he will do things differently. You can't plan everything. After all, what is so awful? — so he's not training to be an Alim, but he's educated, he's clean!"

"And is that all you ask of your son? That he be clean?"

"Maybe, Samad Miah, maybe — "

"And don't speak to me of second generation! One generation! Indivisible! Eternal!"

Somewhere in the midst of this argument, Irie slipped out of the kitchen and headed for the front door. She caught an unfortunate glimpse of herself in the scratch and stain of the hall mirror. She looked like the love child of Diana Ross and Engelbert Humperdinck.

"You have to let them make their own mistakes . . ." came Alsana's voice from the heat of battle, traveling through the cheap wood of the kitchen door and into the hallway, where Irie stood, facing her own reflection, busy tearing out somebody else's hair with her bare hands.

First Morning in Exile

The first morning in exile
It all happened very quickly:
buying a plane ticket
going to the airport
a charter that was late
a three-hour flight.
And then —
a passport officer
confirms my identity
not exactly with goodwill and speed
(in my passport
destroyed cities lurk
and he simply cannot
so early in the morning
on an empty stomach . . .).
His well-fed sleepy fingers
hunt for me through the circuits
of the invisible powerful net
but my face does not appear —
I am still not on the list of those
who want to blow up the world
and after a long search
— resigned and tired
from the night shift
and last night's beer —
he lets me slip into
his blessed world
of short espresso
short memory
and long sound sleep.

ALEKSANDRA DJAJIĆ-HORVÁTH · BOSNIA AND HERZEGOVINA

Aleksandra Djajić-Horváth was born in 1966 in Sarajevo and lived for many years in Bosnia and Herzegovina, but with the outbreak of the war she moved to Novi Sad, Yugoslavia. In 1999, during the NATO bombing campaign, she left that country and moved to Budapest. Since 2001, Aleksandra has been living with her husband in Florence. She has published poems in English and Serbian literary magazines.

GIADA RIPA DI MEANA • ITALY

An Italian who was raised in Brussels and London, Giada Ripa di Meana is a professional photographer who has roamed the world examining dislocation in both public and private space. She holds a master's degree in political science and has been living between New York, Italy, and China for the past six years, both as an artist exhibiting her work and as a photographer for many publications, including *Corriere della Sera, La Repubblica, Io, Donna, Espresso, Sette, Class, Amica,* and *Vanity Fair.*

BELOW AND NEXT PAGE *Lost in Space* series

I am in my late twenties (approaching thirty). I have been able not only to learn many different languages and to travel thoroughly around the world but to explore education and academic systems in four different countries and to work legally in America and Asia and around Europe. Nonetheless, this openness and access to unlimited options (geographical, urban, professional, creative, romantic, et cetera) has thrown me, as well as many other women of my generation, into a difficult decision-making position. I feel that women in their late twenties have been experiencing both strength and confusion — an inner identity quest that is tearing them apart.

ELDA STANCO • VENEZUELA / ITALY

Born and raised in Venezuela with strong ties to her father's Italian heritage, Elda Stanco recently received a doctorate in Hispanic studies from Brown University. She holds dual citizenship (Italian and Venezuelan), has worked in Spain and Venezuela, and is an assistant professor of Spanish at Hollins University in Virginia.

Of Voyages and Broken Borders
Notes on How to Approach Our Generation

"Where are you from?" The inevitable question brings the inevitable answer: "Do you mean . . . where was I born, what are my nationalities, or what is the location of my current residence?" The inevitable response: "Huh?"

Perhaps if you saw me you would understand. People tell me I can pass for Israeli, Chilean, Spanish, Irish, Greek, Brazilian, Iranian. . . . In the beginning it was shocking. Then it became an exciting game of let-the-stranger-guess. It turned funny. A bit neurotic. Eventually it made my stomach hurt, literally. I opted to answer "Nowhere."

Nowadays whoever asks gets the thirty-minute saga of how my existence came about. Word of mouth about me seems to have spread, because fewer and fewer people are asking. But somehow I doubt that the mystery surrounding my "Nowhere" answer has brought this situation about. You see, what I considered to be my characteristic multicultural background, and thus my multicultural "look" (if there is such a thing), is somewhat of a standard for many women today. At first I wondered, Wouldn't this sort of information be in some classified file at an underground government facility? No — others knew about "the file" already. The fashion industry has already capitalized on it, allowing us to look like a geisha one day, a cowgirl the next, and a safari chick for the weekend — all the while not feeling one bit silly.

Undoubtedly, the curiosity over where women are from is being replaced with information sessions about migration patterns. Nowadays what shocks is meeting a woman who has one distinct lineage and hails from one distinct place. A woman who was born, raised, and still lives in the same place and manner as her mother and grandmother is, plainly stated, an oddity. Consequently, many women today are bilingual and trilingual individuals who identify themselves with distinctive traits from diverse cultures, and who can chomp down biryani one night and ceviche the next, all washed down with a solid grappa.

Wouldn't you agree that it has become quite impossible — if not passé — to characterize a woman by her nationality, her ethnicity, her race, or her language? Certainly this generation is best defined as a generation of plurality, of women who cannot and should not be solely classified as German, Southeast Asian, white, or Farsi-speaking. We are "multi-" women: multicultural, multilingual, and multinational — even if that last one sounds like a peacekeeping force.

Our grandmothers and mothers have been immigrants, and so have we. If they voyaged out of necessity, we travel out of need, curiosity, pleasure, and above all, desire. Young adult women today can choose to be at home in more than one locale. We are part of a generation that defies being judged and classified by looks or names. Identity is no longer static and solely inherited. Borders do not truly divide us anymore. *Transatlantic* and *transpacific* are the hot words du jour.

If this is starting to sound too manifesto-y for you, worry not. Behind the irreverent revelry, and despite the jet-set allure that trans- and multi-positions might exude, we are also attempting to

continued

harmonize our cultural baggage. The glamorous facade merely frames the complex issues, emotions, and politics stirred when no single category identifies a woman. How can you juggle speaking Russian at home, English at school, and French on the street? How do you negotiate a hypertraditional southern Italian heritage with a fast-track career? How can you connect with your Filipino ancestry while considering your blonde friends the best of the bunch? The task is not easy; many times it's fun, on occasion it's not. I place my money on new feminist outlooks emerging from this struggle — ideas that will allow second- and third-wave feminists to sit together and make it through a five-course dinner.

My voyage is not the only one in my generation; I have met more and more women with voices like mine, women who know that our generation is transcending borders. Here are some of their stories.

INTERVIEWS WITH "MULTI-" WOMEN

Andreea was born in Romania and grew up in Connecticut. She knows as much about Transylvania as she does about Stamford. She gives the best sale-hunting tips and yet is quick to outline why food in the United States is not really food. Life with her is fast-paced, at times schizophrenic. A conversation with her can be about 80 percent in English, 20 percent in "Sparomitalian" (a cocktail of Spanish, Romanian, and Italian). Andreea's mother escaped Communism and has the scars to prove it. Andreea is her living proof: whatever opportunities her mother never had, Andreea has seized. She has become a lawyer without fear of rejection or of being one of the few. Andreea does what she likes because she can, because her generation is determined to do something about hunger and violence in the United States, Sierra Leone, Congo, and Colombia. "I see women who have arrived and who are not intending to leave anytime soon. I see their mothers swell with pride and even follow suit on a few tucked-away dreams of their own," she concludes.

Suzannah's classic high school tale resounds in every school across the United States: the popular blondes sat at one table, and no one could go near them. They were beautiful, asked out by the guys, and very, very blonde. Suzannah did not sit at this table. Her place was at the table with people who shared her heritage. Somehow, I just know that the blondes argued that the people at Suzannah's table were very heritage-y. Though Suzannah's mother worried when her daughter left the Midwest for the East Coast, she cheered when Suzannah wrote an award-winning story about how multicultural teenagers in the younger generation live. Suzannah knows that a key aspect of the "multi-" life may be a fine equilibrium between the many parts.

Veronika possesses a fame that precedes her. It is not often that you meet a Russian-born woman who grew up in Eastern Europe and Canada and who prefers to spend her free time in Spain. For her, Barcelona feels as homey as Montreal. Veronika's food selections are eclectic: dinner might include a chicken stir-fry, a Russian salad, a New York–style cheesecake, and a bottle of bubbly Italian wine — and it might be followed by salsa lessons. To some this might seem too hectic or too exotic, but to Veronika it is a lifestyle.

The common denominators among Andreea, Suzannah, and Veronika are the freedom and ability to move through borders and identities. All three recognize they are living and creating a world that former generations could only imagine. While not all might agree that the world today is a global village, there is a growing consensus that the living arena women are forging is not based on nationality, race, ethnicity, or language. We are a generation of pluralists, unafraid to turn obsolete categories on their heads and spin them. Women are living and working at such a speedy rate that our own current ideas will soon be passé for us. As for myself . . . well, you would have to give me that "Huh?" before I narrated the thirty-minute transatlantic saga. . . .

MELANIA MESSINA · ITALY

Melania Messina is passionately engaged in influencing the social, economic, and cultural setting of Sicily, where she was born and lives. Her photographs are included in several exhibits and books, and she was chosen to participate in the Culture 2000 program (2000–2006) under the European Commission.

BELOW *Elizabeta from Nigeria Beneath the Western Sky*

I have been amazed by immigrant women's extraordinary energy and will to live despite the difficulties of their conditions. I choose to photograph only women because it seems to me that they have the most responsibility to integrate into the community and the most difficulty doing so. They take care of the children and their education, while trying to preserve the customs and values of their original culture. They often have to break with some of their traditions and start working, sometimes being the only source of income for the entire family. While I was photographing women for my exhibit, I was also interviewing them, and somehow it seemed to me that the portraits needed some fragments of their conversation to be complete. For the exhibit, the images had fragments of the interviews as captions.

"I mainly feel like a foreigner. I am a foreigner among Italians, but I am also a foreigner among my own people."

I will call my children mestiza

I will call my children mestiza
Their father is white
Under the heading "their father is white"
He is part Scot, part native, part john wayne, part
  beatnik
He can carry a card and get minority scholarships
I tell him we need the money
He points to his blond hair and blue eyes and laughs
No one will believe him
So he will be white and privileged
Even though he is neither

I will call my children mestiza
Their mother is brown
Under the heading "their mother is brown"
A privileged, unmarked body
No color, no gender, no race, no religion
The queen was the queen of the entire family but me
I hold my head up with pride

Generations of old Sinhalese blood and Portuguese
colonists and artists and scholars run through the body
that is now brown and third world
Underprivileged and colored
Even though I am neither

I will call my children mestiza
Because they will be called mixed, biracial, multiracial,
racial, racial, racial
I could call them *sudda,* which we now think is affectionate
Sinhalese for whitey, but fifty years ago we spat
it out onto the tarred roads the British built for us

I could call them "buck and tan" like my uncle does to
anyone who is "half and half" after the dark brown and
light brown oxford shoes he had as a child

I will call my children mestiza because their white father
and their brown mother don't believe in categories.

KUMARINI SILVA • SRI LANKA

Born in Sri Lanka, Kumarini Silva has spent the last ten years in the United States and currently lives in Illinois with her husband. A writer and scholar, she teaches film criticism.

REBECCA WALKER • USA

Rebecca Walker is the author of the international bestseller *Black, White and Jewish: Autobiography of a Shifting Self* (Riverhead Books) and the editor of *What Makes a Man: 22 Writers Imagine the Future* (Riverhead Books) and *To Be Real: Telling the Truth and Changing the Face of Feminism* (Anchor/Doubleday). In 1997 Rebecca co-founded the Third Wave Foundation, the only national, philanthropic organization for women aged fifteen to thirty that supports young women's health, education, and activism. When she was twenty-five, *Time* magazine named Rebecca one of fifty future leaders of America. Rebecca graduated with honors from Yale University and is currently at work on a second memoir and a third anthology. She divides what time she has left after giving birth to her son, Tenzin, between New York City and Northern California. Her mother is the prominent African American writer Alice Walker.

Black, White, and Jewish
[An Excerpt]

When I am in college I travel with my mother and also alone to Greece, England, Ireland, Spain, France, Holland. In Spain people tell me I must be a "dirty Mexican" because I don't speak Spanish with the lisp left over from a king, and in France I am treated like the Algerian I am presumed on many occasions to be.

Waiters ignore me, hotel concierges forget my cleaning or otherwise botch my requests, and cab drivers pass me and my friends on the street without so much as a glance. In England, when I go there with Andrew to visit his relatives in Cornwall, my race is completely unspoken, a subject which is obviously on people's minds but is utterly taboo, as if it represents something beyond words, beyond comprehension. As if not speaking about race, except to spit tersely whenever it does come up that it doesn't matter at all, is proof that the British are tolerant, progressive, accepting.

But when I am in high school and my mother starts to make more money, we travel to Jamaica, Mexico, Bali. We go as tourists, but because my mother is an artist and makes an effort to meet other artists everywhere we go, and because we are people of color who take time to learn as much as we can about the culture we are visiting, and because we treat the people we meet as if they are human beings and not objects there solely to respond to our every whim, we are embraced by people, taken in like family.

In these places, where many of the people have skin the same color as mine and where I am not embroiled in the indigenous racial politics of the day, I get a glimpse of a kind of freedom I have not experienced at home, where I always seem to be waiting for a bomb to drop and where I feel I am always being reminded of the significance, for better or worse, of my racial inheritance. In the race-obsessed United States, my color defines me, tells a story I have not written. In countries of color I feel that I am defined by my interactions with people. How open am I, how willing to truly see and be seen by another? What skills do I bring?

How able am I to communicate, even when we speak a different language?

My lover asks me late one night, when we are all bundled up and close under our comforter and our child has long since gone to be with his grandparents for the summer, what it feels like to have white inside of me. What does it feel like to have white inside of you, she asks, and I can hear the burning curiosity in her voice. Physically, you mean? Yeah, physically. Are you aware that there is white in you and does that whiteness feel different from blackness? What is it like to have thin curly hair and lighter skin, what does it feel like?

Her question throws me, but only for a few seconds. My first response is, What is whiteness? And how can one "feel white" when race is just about the biggest cultural construct there is? She nods, she's heard me deconstruct it all a million times. Yeah, yeah, yeah, but if you're operating within it, come on, let yourself go, do you ever feel anything

continued

different? Well, I say. The only time I "feel white" is when black folks point out something in me that they don't want to own in themselves and so label "white." My tendency to psychoanalyze, for example, or my greater tolerance for cold. My hard-earned sense of entitlement is another example, or my insistence on physical beauty wherever I live, which, ironically, comes from the black side of my family tree.

I also "feel white" when I compare myself physically to darker people and find myself lacking. I most experience whiteness, then, as a lack of some attribute or another. A lack of a certain kind of thickness, of a particular full, round, "womanly" shape that I find beautiful and associate with abundance. A lack of color, of the richness, depth, and luminosity that I see in skin darker than my own. A lack of a nonneurotic quality, a kind of freedom from obsessive mental anguish, which I admit I definitely lack, thanks to the Jewish folks in my life.

I don't exactly think to myself, *Oh I feel white*, at those particular moments, but I do carry a constant sense of not black in those areas, of deprivation in those areas, of wanting to have more of something other than what I have. But is whiteness something I can feel on or in my body like a stomachache or a burn? No.

I ask her if she feels black. Yes is her instant reply. And because her mother was so color conscious, all her life associating goodness with lighter-skinned black people and evil with those darker, and because she went to one of the most color-stratified black colleges in the country and because dark skin is generally reviled in a culture that deifies whiteness, she says she feels an instant kinship with those who are darker, who share her brownness, who have been raised with the same shit hurled at them, the same messages to have to rewrite. She feels black, all of the time.

She says, on the tail end of all that, So like when someone black starts talking about "my people" have been oppressed for so long, do you identify with those people? Do you feel that bond in your gut, can you throw your fist up behind that? Do you think of black people as your people?

I sense we are headed into a danger zone. Is this a test? I breathe. I do and don't, I say. I was never granted the luxury of being claimed unequivocally by any people or "race," and so when someone starts talking about "my people" I know that if we look hard enough or scratch at the surface long enough, they would have some problem with some part of my background, the part that's not included in the "my people" construction. It's not that I am not loved and accepted by friends and family, it is just that there is always the thing that sets me slightly apart, the "cracker" lurking in my laugh.

And then there is the question of how I can feel fully identified with "my people" when I have other people, too, who are not included in that grouping. And this feeling I have, of having other people, too, is in effect even though the other people under consideration do not claim me. Does that make sense? I ask. She nods.

What I do feel is an instant affinity with beings who suffer, whether they are my own, whatever that means or not. Do I identify with the legacy of anti-Jewish sentiment and exclusion? Yes. Do I identify with the internment of Japanese-Americans during World War II? Yes. Do I identify with the struggle against brutality and genocide waged against the Native Americans in this country? Yes. Do I feel I have to choose one of these allegiances in order to know who I am or in order to pay my proper respect to my ancestors? No. Do I hope that what my ancestors love in me is my ability to muster compassion for those who suffer, including myself? Yes.

It seems to me that this, too, is how memory works. What we remember of what was done to us shapes our view, molds us, sets our stance. But what we remember is past, it no longer exists, and yet still we hold on to it, live by it, surrender so much control to it. What do we become when we put down the scripts written by history and memory, when each person before us can be seen free of the cultural or personal narrative we've inherited or devised?

When we, ourselves, can taste that freedom?

PIREENI SUNDARALINGAM • SRI LANKA / UNITED KINGDOM

Pireeni Sundaralingam was born in Sri Lanka and educated at Oxford. Her poetry has been published in a number of anthologies, including the *Oxford and Cambridge Anthology of Poetry* (1992). She is a professor of cognitive science, and her new album, *Bridge Across the Blue,* examines themes of identity and migration through poetry and music. Pireeni currently lives in the United States.

Evening

Because evening is not just the end of the day
but the drawing together of death's dark forces

because night is a place through which shadows stalk
and a dynasty of our ghosts still wanders

because I am the daughter of your only daughter
when our sons are all dead and the names
of our living have been scattered,

you will weave these Dark Time prayers for me
pour water, biting like steel, through my fingers
place ash, sacred, between my eyes.

Grandmother,
holding a house whose rooms have been emptied,
where the heirlooms have vanished

and the photographs of our men
are garlanded with silence,

you will light these camphor lamps for me,
chant mantras that pull down planets,

name stars that will stay faithful,
following my footsteps
even into exile

2003 marked the twentieth anniversary of the Sri Lankan civil war, a war that has led to sixty thousand deaths and a million people sent into diaspora. Through telling my story I hope to tell the stories of all the other Sri Lankan women of my generation who have seen nothing other than war and exile in their lifetimes.

I also seek to relate the universality of our experience. We live in a time when ethnic conflict has led to the simultaneous decimation of numerous communities across the world. While the nature of such brutality is not new in terms of world history, the sheer scale of such bloodshed may well be unique to our generation. Nevertheless, thanks to advances in communication technology over the last decade, there has never been such a chance for us to grasp, at a grassroots level, the similarities of our respective struggles and to build bridges between all our struggling communities.

There is a Sufi fable about a group of people called the islanders. These people live on an island for years and years under fear and strict rule. They are not allowed to explore the water around their island, so they live in continuous fear of what's beyond the horizon. Then one day they become enlightened and courageous, build a boat, and go together to explore what lies beyond their shores.

The Sufis believe that this fable is a parable of the human mind and spirit, unwilling at first to expand and explore. The calligraphy in red across the face you see here is the fable written in Arabic, with the letters and words actually depicting the boat and the islanders paddling.

I've used this particular story in my self-portrait, entitled *20 Years* (by the way, this self-portrait consists of two pieces, *Self Portrait 1983* and *Self Portrait 2003*, hence *20 Years*) because I am an Iranian woman in the Diaspora. There is no blueprint or map set up for me as an Iranian woman who grew up in Germany and the United States. We children of the Diaspora are in a peculiar position of not belonging to one world or another.

From the day I left Iran in 1984 at the age of eight, I have never been home again or had a home again. Even more interesting is that even if I could return to Iran today I would still not be home.

The idea of *home* in the mind of a refugee becomes a distant fetish that is never again attainable and naturally transforms into a longing, a river of delicious sadness that forever lives inside her heart.

ASA SOLTAN RAHMATI • IRAN

Asa Soltan Rahmati was born in Ahwaz, Iran, in 1976. The backdrop of her childhood consisted of the Pahlavi dynasty, the Islamic revolution in 1979, and then the almost decade-long war between Iran and Iraq. Asa and her family fled to Germany in 1984 and lived there as political refugees for eight years before once more seeking political asylum, this time in the United States. Her politics are personal, and her artistic work draws on her life as a refugee.

ABOVE *20 Years*

LAURA BOUSHNAK • PALESTINE

Laura Boushnak, a Palestinian photographer educated in Kuwait and Lebanon, works at the Middle East head-quarters of Agence France-Presse in Cyprus. Her work focuses on the refugee experience.

BELOW *Struggle*

I was born a third-generation Palestinian refugee and raised in a traditional family in conservative Kuwait. As a refugee, I have no passport, which makes foreign travel difficult. When I was thirteen, I endured a year of chaos due to the 1990 Iraqi invasion of Kuwait. My father decided we would stay put because our only other option was to go to Lebanon, where the civil war was still raging.

After high school, my father could not afford to send me abroad to study (foreigners in Kuwait are generally barred from the state university, and there is no private college education). So I worked as a receptionist, earning a meager salary in a job that required minimal intelligence. I knew I deserved better.

Determined not to remain trapped, I enrolled in a correspondence program through the Lebanese University to study social sciences. At the same time, I started a distance-learning course through the New York Institute of Photography. With the help of books, movies, and Arab and Western friends, I broadened my horizons. My curiosity for a better life allowed me to overcome the obstacles I faced. At age twenty, I left Kuwait and went to Beirut to finish my degree and start a career in the male-dominated world of photojournalism.

Immigration is a big challenge. Leaving the country where you were born, starting everything from scratch in a new place, and communicating in a language that is not your mother tongue — this is never easy. What can be found in this painting is a woman sitting at her window. The window is bright with a feeling of hope, but the sky is red with lots of images. These images symbolize difficulties we have experienced, such as war, revolution, and losing religion and family. In this painting there are lots of people around, but none are close.

NEGAR POOYA · IRAN

Negar Pooya, who was born in Tehran in 1971, is a painter and printmaker. She completed a master's degree in graphics, and she has exhibited her works in Iran, Canada, Japan, Romania, and the United States.

RIGHT *Disconnection*

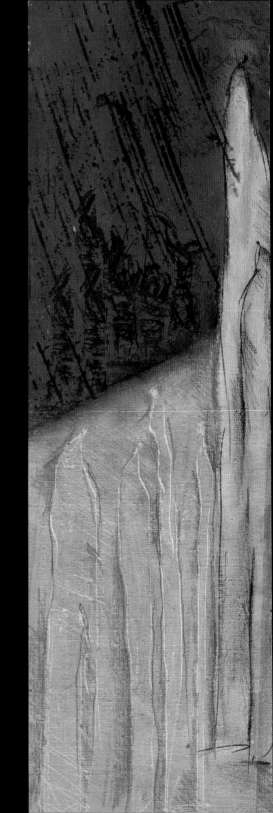

Le Au Giusila

[An Excerpt from *Where We Once Belonged*]

Our *'aiga* was the first in Malaefou to get a TV, even if it was black and white, and most kids said it didn't count and that Mu's *'aiga* was actually the first since they had it colored and clearer, and much, much larger than ours.

We got the TV from New Zealand via my grandmother's brother's son, Masapati, who bought it from an American family who lived there in New Zealand. Our relatives thought it better to send the TV to us in Samoa . . . in Malaefou.

That week, before the TV arrived, everyone wanted to be our friends.

Fiafia and Faanoano — twins who were six months older than me, and who never spoke to me directly, but teased me about bringing leftovers to school and wearing panties with the Dunlop tire rubber waist and that I peed in bed until I was nine — suddenly gave wide smiles whenever we met. The kind of smiles you see at stores on Santa Claus at Christmas, or on a girl with yellow hair and white teeth on the side of a box of toothpaste. They would offer pencils at pastor's school whenever the eye of my pencil died. They would offer a sharpener to resurrect the eye of the pencil. They would offer to comb and *fili* my hair in a style they knew I did not know. They would say *"ku-lou"* whenever they passed me — even though they were older. And told me their deep, deep secrets — that they stole cigarettes from Leaga, their father, who

never suspected them, and that their father would beat Epenesa, their brother, up for it; that they cheated on the Sunday School Final; that they saw Donna the *fa'afafige* "do it" to Leauvaa, who is supposed to be sick for girls only.

In addition, they invited me once to sleep over at their house and offered me the cleanest and prettiest sheets, the biggest pillow with "Jesus is the Reason" pillowcase. And I was allowed to use the Palmolive soap first before they washed their hair. This was a luxury, for my family washed only with Fasimoli Ka Mea, laundry soap.

Their mother asked me that night if I could ask Pisa to send someone over when *Fantasy Island* came on. I told her that I would, and that I would run over personally, and that she should stay also for *Days of Our Lives*.

"They're unmasking Roman tonight!"

She said she would stay on and that I was a good girl, a fine influence on her daughters. But she also said that I should try to stay away from that Lili.

"She's too old to hang around you girls, isn't

SIA FIGIEL • SAMOA

Sia Figiel, often described as Samoa's first woman novelist and hailed as "the voice of the Pacific Islands," was born in the Samoan village of Matautu Tai in 1967. Her first book, *Where We Once Belonged* (Kaya Press, 1999), won the prestigious Commonwealth Writers' Prize Best First Book award for the South East Asia and South Pacific region. Sia has been on extensive reading tours; recent travels have taken her to New Zealand, Australia, Hawaii, Los Angeles, London, and Germany, as well as to several international literary festivals.

she? You can sleep over whenever you want . . . whenever your father allows."

Everyone was too excited the night the TV arrived. We all knew its history before we even saw it: that it was an American TV bought from an American couple by Misipaki and that it was arriving here to make Malaefou history. Before the TV arrived, kids were already choosing what they wanted to see:

Charlie's Angels;
The Bionic Woman;
Star Trek;
Big Time Wrestling.

The elders were already saying that everyone in school should go to bed when the *Love Boat* came on, which was fine with all of us. Who wanted to see a bald-headed captain steering a ship full of morons around anyway?

That night, after the evening meal (which was early and quick), everyone rushed to the front of the house. Kids were fighting and pulling hair — and pulling more hair — over who would get to be closer to the TV.

"You should all move back," said Asu, my father's brother, who thinks he owns everything in the house . . . even though he's unemployed, and never went to school, and has no kids of his own (who

would want to marry him?), and is big, and has a big voice, and rules us like a dog rules cats.

"Not too close or you'll go blind! No one is to touch the TV, understand? No one. Any of you kids caught touching the TV is going to be wrapped up in their sheets and thrown out into the *paepae*. Do you understand?"

We nodded our heads, too excited to listen. We just wanted to see moving pictures.

After Asu finished explaining the TV rules, he plugged it in and switched it on. Nothing came out. He took the plug out and tried it again, but still nothing happened.

"Where are the pictures?" we all asked. "Where are the pictures?"

Faleniu, our neighbor, who works for the Public Works in Apia, came over to the TV and spoke to Asu.

"That the TV won't work without an antenna or a transformer."

"What are those?"

While Faleniu explained to Asu and to all the older boys and men of the *fale* who were gathering

continued

now around the TV what a transformer was and why American stuff would not work here in Malaefou, the women of the house (half-disappointed, half-embarrassed) were heard shouting.

"Damn those New Zealanders!"

"Damn that Misipaki!"

"Bake him in an oven!"

"Bake them all in an oven!"

"Damn! Damn! Damn!"

The village children cried.

"Your TV is broken!"

"Your relatives in New Zealand are not rich enough to send a TV that works!"

Three months later Filiga found an antenna and transformer. Mr. Brown was returning to his Australia, and wanted to sell his antenna and transformer for 250 tala. Filiga borrowed the money at work, which meant we would have to take leftovers to school . . . forever.

The actual antenna and transformer, sent by the relatives in New Zealand, was recovered later (much, much later) at Valu's house.

Valu was the Customs Inspector and had confiscated a refrigerator from American Samoa that he was using to make ice and other things.

'AIGA-FILIGA was marked in large bright red capital letters on the bottom of the transformer Valu had been using and using for months now.

Eseese the secretary noticed this and notified the men of our family, but only after Valu told her he loved his wife and was going back to her. The men of our family approached Valu with heavy fists and threats and all. In which case, Valu offered them a ham, two cans of *pisupo*, and an umbrella for the old lady.

"Never do this again! Understand? Never!"

This after many angry letters flew between New Zealand and Samoa.

The relative in New Zealand wrote:

"You should have been happy! You were the first family to have a TV that came all the way from America to Misipaki, who spent all his pay and sweat to buy it for you . . . and an antenna . . . and a transformer."

The relatives in Malefou were bitter at the relatives in New Zealand for sending something that didn't work and replied back:

"How do we know you sent a transformer . . . or an antenna? Why didn't you send them all together?"

"You're so ungrateful!" they wrote from New Zealand.

"You're so stingy!" the relatives here wrote back.

To prove they weren't stingy and that they had our best interests at heart, the New Zealanders sent one hundred New Zealand dollars for the children's *ipu*, for *Le Lotu A Tamaiti* [the day after White Sunday], which was used (more or less) to buy material, taro, kerosene, porridge for Tausi and the babies, Poker or Suipi.

Twenty tala was announced as the 'Aiga Filiga donation on White Sunday. A note was attached to the money:

> *We are all well. We are sad that we couldn't be there to celebrate such a day with the whole family. We are thinking of you all and pray to God that we will see you again, soon.*
>
> *Sale's son, Iopu, is coming to Samoa for Le Loku A Kamaiki. He is bringing lollies for the kids, and shoes for Moe and Sita, and the old lady's white dress.*
>
> *Alofaaga e tele mo outou,*
> *Le Au Giusila.*
>
> *p.s. Please don't tell the old lady about the white dress.*
> *We thought it was better to be prepared. Who knows?*

KAISU KOIVISTO • FINLAND

Born in Seinäjoki, Finland, Kaisu Koivisto is a visual artist whose creative focus has been shaped by the mad cow disease epidemic in Europe in the mid 1990s. Kaisu's sculpture and installations explore the relationship between people and animals. She uses recycled materials and photography to depict these environmental issues, which affect the lives of people in small towns as well as in big cities.

BELOW *Model Airplane (The Nationality of Animals series)*

In my works, I would like to emphasize that the attitudes of many people still reflect the ideas of past centuries — for example, "finders keepers," the belief that nature can be exploited in any possible way. In my work, animals hold deep symbolic meaning, reminding the viewer of the cycle of life. Even our everyday objects will decompose one day, proving that nature is stronger than human attempts to master the universe. I am fascinated by the ways in which people organize the environments they live in, only to discover that the systems can be destroyed by, for example, earthquakes or floods — both of which are, in fact, natural phenomena, part of the ecosystem of the globe. Animal diseases (BSE, foot-and-mouth disease, bird flu), as well as human-related diseases such as AIDS, spread as animal products and people move around the world. Diseases do not respect borders in any way.

The generation of women to which I belong is defined by change. Change and changeability. Born in South Africa and becoming adults at the time of huge social and political change, we are the generation on the cusp.

Childhood belongs to an era that is considered and described as totally separate and apart from the present time. Markers from that time seem like strange relics — familiar but peculiar: Am I that girl on the beach who never saw a black person all holiday and was told it was because "blacks don't like water"?

Our late teens and early twenties found us reeling during a time of upheaval and confusion — self-discovery linked to newly discovered social realities, broken family relationships, and wild struggles for self-expression amid political struggle and erupting communities.

As an independent adult woman, I see us walking across the battlefields of devastated personal relationships and fractured lives and picking at bits and things that seem to have life left in them that we can hold, remold, adapt, breathe love into. . . .

My generation of women come together from deeply divergent pasts to sticky-tape and bandage a society wounded by itself. In each other's eyes we see pain and longing and confusion and hope and joy. Mostly I see us as the menders. Nothing is constant. Adaptation is essential. Taking on the challenges of change: nurturing our collective children, the younger generation, with values of caring and self-love and respect for all. And growing ourselves as precious individuals.

ERIKA HIBBERT · SOUTH AFRICA

Erika Hibbert graduated in 1989 from the University of the Witwatersrand, Johannesburg, receiving the University Merit Award for Painting. Her work has been exhibited at numerous galleries in South Africa and in Europe. In addition to painting and drawing, Erika has worked as a teacher and book illustrator and has been a member of several art committees.

ABOVE *Self Portraits in Namibian Landscapes*

YOLANDA VERA FERRERA • SPAIN

Yolanda Vera Ferrera is a native of Tenerife, one of the Canary Islands of Spain. In her text she presents examples of processes of displacement and migration that many women of her generation worldwide have experienced. The journey begins by reflecting on the experience of gaining and losing autonomy over the course of a trip.

Where the Journey Begins

Where does the journey begin? Mine did not begin when I left Barcelona to go back to Tenerife. Nor later when I left Tenerife for London. It wasn't when I arrived in London either. It began four and a half weeks later, in the hospital.

My feet were burning. A lot. The in-between-my-toes was burning.

All right, my child.

Your whole body was burning!

I went to the hospital because my whole body was burning. I went to the hospital because it was my second panic attack that week.

If I had known at the time how London's healthcare system worked, I would not have felt so comforted by that hospital in Dalston. In that early morning, above all, I guess I just needed to feel recomforted.

My feet were burning. The antihistamine that the nurse gave me didn't seem to be helping me to reconceptualize a painful sensation of displacement. One, two, three, four and a half weeks, and Yolanda has changed in color, scent, and texture.

Cold water, really cold, to stop the burning, to lower the pulse.

The hospital bathrooms: the cold water spigots in the hospital bathrooms were not working. The hospital bar where you get ice: the hospital bar was closed. Go back to the bathrooms, lift the top off the back of the toilet, touch the water inside, climb on top, putting in one foot and then the other. My feet inside the tank of a toilet whose water is cold, very cold.

Two images: a) me standing straight up in the tank of a toilet, looking happy; b) me stooped waaaay over, serving respected millionaires in a yacht club near Bond Street.

It was easier to find myself there — standing with my head peeking over the bathroom door, observing the other women who came in to use the restroom — than to find myself looking for food in the kitchen garbage at the club where I worked.

And that's where my journey began.

Consecutive and contradictory attempts to deconstruct all monolithic inventions of myself had failed since my arrival in London. I had systematically defined myself in terms of my exclusion.

It was hard for me to find spaces where I could remind myself of my privilege. Where I could remember that in the end, I was the one who had decided to leave my island, in spite of resistance from my family.

That day in the hospital I thought of returning to Tenerife. I had a lot of fear and little energy. I was tired of trying to find the words to dignify my daily humiliation at work, which was apparently aimed at teaching me how the foreigner, the non-English speaker, the voiceless should act. . . .

I was not surprised to find my grandmother María in my storm of thoughts. She would never

continued

have put her feet inside a toilet. She had already suffered enough humiliation for not knowing how to read that she would never have put herself in such a ridiculous position.

Sorry, Grandma. I take it back! My grandmother María knows how to read and write. She learned when she was older, before she turned blind. She would have learned much sooner if they hadn't prevented her for so long.

My grandmother María is still alive. The years of poverty didn't kill her, and neither did the harsh work since the age of five. She survived the "fevers" that ended her sister Francisca's life when they went to Cuba to reunite with their father. She did not give up when, as a girl, she was made to marry a man of her mother's choosing; nor did she yield in those three and a half years when she didn't hear from her husband after Franco's army detained him and brought him to Morocco.

How many times did my grandmother bow her head? How many times did she lift it up? *How many journeys did you begin in your lifetime,* abuela?

One of my strategies of resistance was based on the creation of an intellectual discourse that allowed me to observe my own history. It was just what all those years in academia had trained me to do.

My recourse was to imagine that I carried a digital camera with me and was documenting the daily power feuds I felt I was losing.

One time, while I was studying in Barcelona, I approached the girl in charge of the university computer room and asked her which of the three printers in the room worked best. She got up from her chair and called the security guard. "Please, Miss, could you be so kind as to show me your student ID?" "Why? Is there a problem?" "This computer room is only for the students at this school, and as far as I know, we don't have any Latin Americans studying here." "I'm not Latin American, I'm from the Canaries." "What?! I didn't know that Canary Islanders talked like that. I went to Tenerife last summer, and girl, I loved it! Anyway, I'm better now — I thought some Latin American was trying to weasel her way into the university."

I walked barefoot, my wet feet leaving footprints (European size 37) from the bathroom to the chaotic waiting room . . .

And I waited . . .

Nine and a half hours until a male body dressed in scrubs tended to me.

At some point during those nine and a half hours I decided to stay in London.

To begin the journey.

To explore my own narratives about my experience of migration. The contradictory ways in which I represent myself and others represent me. My capacity to survive or to annihilate myself. The moments when I have taken advantage of the privileges granted to me by my European passport or my university education, and the moments when I have searched for points of commonality with other narratives of struggle and resistance.

One, two, three and a half years, and I'm still in London.

Thanks to scholarships and bank loans, I arrived at the department of gender studies at a university in London where I'm studying gender theory. A place where now, as before, I reinvent myself in my search for concrete ways to dream about defeating daily exploitations, both big and small, of which I am also guilty.

It was daytime when I left the hospital. I barely had an hour and a half to get to my house, put on my uniform, and go to the yacht club near Bond Street. . . .

[FROM THE ORIGINAL SPANISH]

Y allí empezó mi viaje.

Consecutivos y contradictorios intentos de destabilizar cualquier monolítica construccíon de mi misma habían fracasado desde mi llegada a Londrés. Sistemáticamente me había definido monoliticamente en términos de exclusión.

4

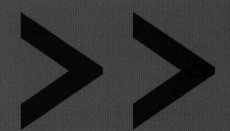

TOWARDS

SO HERE WE

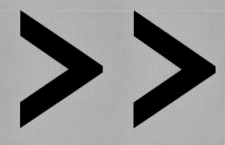

ARE.

At the start of a century. Connected across continents. With résumés full of experience, passports full of stamps, and in-boxes full of messages from scattered friends and loved ones.

The newspaper is full of tragedy and gloom. War. Disease. Environmental destruction. Our parents and grandparents, and even our friends, are asking, "What's becoming of this planet?"

And yet, somehow, there's also a sense of imminent juncture. Of this moment that's arriving, this brief flash in time that has been years in the making, after centuries in which the roles of women have been constantly changing. This moment where we, as a generation, get to take our place at the table. And join the conversation. And say:

Yes, we know how it has been, and how hard it has been to get here. But listen, here's where we want to steer the ship.

We are a generation of women who are more globally interconnected than ever before. And we can use that connection to inspire each other, to bounce ideas off one another, to create common visions and strategies. We are a generation of women with more access to education, work opportunities, and new and alternative lifestyle choices than any generation in history. We can use those privileges to effect real change in our own lives and the lives of those around us.

The selections in this chapter provide fun, dynamic entry points into that conversation about the future. They tackle a variety of issues, from the environment to armed conflict. However, what unites these entries is not the specific issues they address but the self-confidence of their authors and artists. It is their willingness to dream of something beyond what may seem possible now, their belief in their own voices and visions, and their courage to put those voices out there in the world.

More than anything else, it is this spirit of confidence that characterizes our generation of women. And this same spirit will enable us to make an impact on the world. The young women in this chapter are joyful, humorous, positive, and dynamic. They have beautiful words and beautiful faces. They represent our future.

And so do you.

Being
a
Woman
Is
a
Natural
Act

An everyday impulse
that gives you direction
And you must follow
where it may go
always
With its beauty
and unsteadiness

With passion
In the day to day
A personal will
To want. To feel. To live
With the sun
Until the end.

[FROM THE ORIGINAL SPANISH]

Ser mujer es un acto natural

Un impulso diario
Que te marca dirección
Y debes seguirla
Hasta donde sea
Siempre
Con sus bellezas
Y caidas

Con pasión
En el día a día
Una fuerza personal
Querer. Sentir. Vivir
Con el sol
Hasta el fin

SER

ER ES UN ACTO NATURAL

This photographic project makes use of the familiar aesthetic of images from fashion magazines to present the real lives of women. I use images representing daily life in order to reclaim the ideas that fashion sells us. These images are the result of everyday moments among a group of women friends between the ages of twenty-one and twenty-eight, hanging out and expressing themselves naturally in front of the camera.

With this I try to convey the simple and intriguing life of any woman who is simply herself, without commercial or social stereotypes. We need not adjust our self-perception or desires to the path laid out for us; we can create our own. This is a kind of anti-publicity that does not offer ideas to buy, but rather ideas to live by.

In Mexican culture, a woman is raised for matrimony, to assist a man as a secretary, an aide, an employee, a cashier, a manager, a wife. Many of my friends' mothers are housewives, and their social participation is now limited to memories and yearnings from grammar school and high school. Their studies were truncated by pregnancies and matrimonies. Their aspirations are archived in letters to childhood friends, saved within old records and magazine cutouts. And they are the women who formed us; their minds and examples showed us what it means to be a woman and the way a woman should behave.

But the history of these women has pushed us to question the path to follow. After seeing my mother's life, I have had the strength to take control of my own life, to cling to my decisions and desires, whatever the price. Through questioning her and other women of her generation, I have known clearly how we must act socially. These women have advanced the answers that lead us to demand our place, to rob spaces, to shout louder until we are listened to as women, people, thinking beings who have much to contribute and to say.

In my experience, being a woman has not created any additional obstacles in my professional life. But this world is the scene of great fighting — nothing is simply handed out; if you want something, you need to get it for yourself. Nothing comes easily; everything that you wish for must be planted and tended on a daily basis. That is also how it is for all women. With our day-to-day actions, we must demonstrate what we are and what we can do. We must have something to offer, so we must first work internally, constructing who we are and what we want to give to the world.

In this sense, being a woman is a constant challenge that requires our active participation. We have a new vision, a new perspective to offer the world. And I believe that my generation no longer has an excuse for not doing so. The walls have been destroyed. The doors are now open. It is up to us to determine what to do and what path to take.

ITZEL MARTÍNEZ DEL CAÑIZO FERNÁNDEZ • MEXICO

Itzel Martínez del Cañizo Fernández was born in Mexico City in 1978 but considers Tijuana to be her home — a border city, a constant crossover point from Latin America to the United States — that gives her an almost infinite universe of themes to explore in audiovisual formats. She has worked as a university professor, has developed courses for children and district officials, and now codirects an independent art production company called YonkeART.

RIGHT AND PRECEDING PAGE *Ser mujer es un acto natural (Being a Woman Is a Natural Act)*

MANAL AL-DOWAYAN • SAUDI ARABIA

Manal Al-Dowayan holds a bachelor's degree in management information systems and a master's degree in systems analysis and design. Currently, Manal works for a Saudi Arabian oil company and freelances as a photographer in her spare time. Her photographs focus on women and the environments that surround them.

LEFT *An Angel Dances*

A Woman Is a Woman Although

A woman is a woman although.
Words and shapes do not comprise the content.
A woman can be a skill
A rib or a defect.
A woman overflows the edges
Measures up
Eases the dissonance
She plays with the organ and rings the bell.
A woman can be a scream
A belly
A precipice.
A woman can be an abyss or a haven.
And she can be both
And she is.

Uma mulher é uma mulher ainda que

Uma mulher é uma mulher ainda que.
Palavras e formas não comportam o conteúdo.
Uma mulher pode ser um jeito
Uma costela ou um defeito.
Uma mulher transborda pelos cantos
Enche as medidas
Contorna o desafino
Toca punheta e toca sino.
Uma mulher pode ser um grito
Uma barriga
Um precípicio.
Uma mulher pode ser um abismo ou um porto
E pode ser os dois
E é.

[FROM THE ORIGINAL PORTUGESE]

MARIA REZENDE • BRAZIL

Maria Rezende is a poet from Rio de Janeiro. She is profoundly influenced by the art of reciting poetry and has released several spoken-word albums. Her work addresses the connections between language, femininity, and female desires. Maria has also published one book of poetry entitled *Substantivo feminino* (*The Feminine Subject*).

AYA DE LEÓN • USA

Aya de León is an African American/Puerto Rican artist, activist, and teacher who lives in the San Francisco Bay Area. In 2001 she toured the United States with her one-woman hip-hop theater show, *Thieves in the Temple: The Reclaiming of Hip Hop.* The poem below is recorded on her first spoken-word album, *Aya de León: Live at La Peña.*

If Women Ran Hip Hop

If women ran hip hop
the beats and rhymes would be just as dope,
but there would never be a bad vibe when you walked in the place
and the clubs would be beautiful and smell good
and the music would never be too loud
but there would be free earplugs available anyway
and venues would have skylights and phat patios
and shows would run all day not just late at night
cuz If women ran hip hop we would have nothing to be ashamed of
and there would be an African marketplace
with big shrines to Oya
Yoruba deity of the female warrior and entrepreneur
and women would sell and barter and prosper

If women ran hip hop
there would never be shootings
cuz there would be onsite conflict mediators
to help you work through all that negativity and hostility
and there would also be free condoms and dental dams
in pretty baskets throughout the place
as well as counselors to help you make the decision:
do I really want to have sex with him or her?
and there would be safe, reliable, low-cost 24-hour transportation home
and every venue would have on-site quality child care
where kids could sleep while grown folks danced
and all shows would be all ages cause the economy of hip hop wouldn't revolve around the sale of
alcohol

If women ran hip hop
same gender–loving and transgender emcees
would be proportionally represented
and get mad love from everybody
and females would dress sexy if we wanted to celebrate our bodies
but it wouldn't be that important because
everyone would be paying attention to our minds, anyway

If women ran hip hop
men would be relieved because it's so draining
to keep up that front of toughness and power and control 24-7

If women ran hip hop
the only folks dancing in cages would be dogs and cats
from the local animal shelter
excited about getting adopted by pet lovers in the crowd

If women ran hip hop
there would be social workers available to refer gangsta rappers
to 21-day detox programs where they could get clean and sober
from violence and misogyny

but best of all, if women ran hip hop
we would have the dopest female emcees ever
because all the young women afraid to bust
would unleash their brilliance on the world

cause it's the time for the reclaiming of hip hop.

MARÍA ADELA DÍAZ • GUATEMALA

María Adela Díaz is a graphic designer and artist who was born in Guatemala in 1973. She now resides in California. Her art expresses the essence and sublimity of women. She aims to seduce nature within an everyday context and attempts to transform the observer into a part of her own work.

I chose some pages out of my diary as part of my work relating to my experience in the United States. Since I have no space to show my work in, my diary has served as a place to record my reactions to my days in exile. A diary is personal. By making it public and showing women of my generation puzzle pieces from my life, I hope to inspire and intrigue.

Here is my wish for this world:

I hope each of us finds his or her personal guide or master. This does not have to be a guru or a religious figure, but simply a person whom we respect and can look up to for guidance and advice — perhaps our parents, a schoolteacher, a relative, or simply a good friend.

I also hope we each learn to deal with the negative voice inside us in a constructive way on a daily basis, so that we can see behind our own illusions but still have dreams to hope for.

BETTINA SALOMON · AUSTRIA

Bettina Salomon was born in Austria and has traveled extensively in Asia and Europe. She lived and worked in London for eight years and in San Francisco for one year. Her passion and love are photography and her son, Eliah, who was born in September 2004.

LEFT *Pink and Blue*

Kôtè Don
[TRANSLATED FROM THE ORIGINAL BAMBARA]

Young people of the city.
Smart young girls,
This song is for you.
You who are everything that is dynamic.
Let us rejoice.
Let's dance the *kôtè,*
Youth will pass,
So make the most of it.

My joie de vivre is taken for shamelessness,
My thirst for change for pretension,
Faced with my curiosity, my quest for the new,
Conservative minds spread slander,
And question everything that
My times are about.
But don't listen to malicious gossip
It would be a waste of time.
Youth is ephemeral,
Let's celebrate and dance the *kôtè.*

Ever changing, I dislike what is rigid, set,
What "is" without knowing why,
All that is hierarchical, static.
I respect my ancestors,
But tradition is not infallible,

It is not absolute,
Time passes, we all change,
Nothing remains the same.

This is for you, young people,
Let's dance the *kôtè.*

Let's make the most of our time, let's celebrate.

From philosophy to science,
Biology to history,
I master the knowledge transmitted to me.
Nevertheless,
The elders reproach me for my curiosity.
But it is true that I am the tightrope walker,
Perched high on a wire
Overlooking disparity:
The encounter between the culture of my
   ancestors,
Where knowledge is transmitted in secret,
Where the unsaid is fundamental,
Since the word is sacred;
And that of my modern education,
Where nothing that is thought is inexpressible.

ROKIA TRAORÉ • MALI

Rokia Traoré is an exciting and bright new musical talent from West Africa. She received widespread acclaim in 1998 for her poignant debut album, *Mouneïssa.* She makes music as someone who has grown up listening to American and European music — jazz, classical, rock, and pop. Though inspired by many forms of music, her own is not fusion. Her most recent album, *Bowmboï,* was recorded in her native Mali on traditional instruments. Rokia has also traveled to San Francisco to record two tracks with the world-class strings of the Kronos Quartet.

ABOVE Lyrics to "Kôtè Don" from the album *Bowmboï*

SARAH JONES • USA

Sarah Jones is an Obie Award–winning playwright, actor, and poet. Her acclaimed solo shows include *Surface Transit, Women Can't Wait,* and *Bridge and Tunnel,* for which she has received several distinctions, including a Helen Hayes Award, HBO's Comedy Arts Festival's Best One Person Show Award, and two Drama Desk nominations. She has performed for the United Nations, the Supreme Court of Nepal, and members of the U.S. Congress. She resides in New York with her partner, Steve Colman.

girls&women

they have built prisons
for us

at night we cup our words to our mouths and
drink before they
come to dry the day

they have built networks
for us

our messages dart electric out
into a world that is naked
burning at the edges
in the center, too

they have built history
for us

in secret we record our names
in the lines of our palms
write "freedom" in smoke
as their flames lick our soles

but we are clay that cools
hardens only on the outside
we count the stars that represent us
innumerable, eternal

we are limbs regrown
springing up along the ground
into the dust among the
mines and mortar
we laugh and there is a glint they might mistake for
diamonds in our teeth

but it is water and it belongs to us

Growing Roots

If a tree grows and it is cut away from its roots, then that tree will die. This is something I really believe.

When I was sixteen, I won the gold medal in figure skating at the 1994 Olympic Winter Games in Lillehammer, Norway. I was the first Ukrainian gold medalist after the fall of the Soviet Union. I was a tree with branches growing tall and strong. I was on top of the world. Many people know this story. They know how I lost my mother to ovarian cancer when I was thirteen and how my father left us when I was two. They know how much determination it took me to get through those events, to go to America and train, and then finally, to get the gold.

What they don't know is the story of how I became an adult, the story of how I developed a full life that wasn't just about professional success, the story of how I grew my roots.

What do you do after you're a gold medalist? You're flying high, and then what? First I had to make the transition to professional skating — which was hard because it was more about performing and entertaining than about precision and technical skill. I was sixteen, and my body started changing shape, just as you might predict for a girl that age — but no one told me what to expect, or what I needed to eat to maintain fitness for my skating. And life in America, wow! There was low-carb this and low-fat that and sugar-free this and a million options for everything you ever wanted to buy. I didn't know what to do — so I entertained myself by buying and trying everything.

For years, it was just me and the entertaining, and there was no one else in my life. I'd go on tour with all the skaters, who were my friends, and then I'd come home, and it was just me, alone, in my apartment. I didn't really trust a lot of people. There were always lots of people around, but they were being paid by me. I started drinking a lot. My doctor told me I had a problem with alcohol. Olympic champions don't have any problems, you know? They're just supposed to go out there and skate. At least that's what the magazines tell you.

But then when I was about twenty-three, things started changing. I somehow knew I couldn't spend the rest of my life concentrating only on the skating. There was more to being a person than that, and I had to be ready and willing to find it.

One day during the holiday season that year, a friend invited me to a Christmas party. I didn't want to go, but she forced me to. And this guy, Gene, was there, and he was so fun to talk to, and so nice. . . .

We're now engaged.

Gene took a lot of my fear away. Creating a life with him gave me the opportunity to spread my wings outside the public eye, to take time off from touring, to enjoy small things, like going to the grocery store and cooking dinner, to relax and be myself. Before that, every time I went to a restaurant, all I could pay attention to was playing the part for people who asked me for autographs. Now, I have a personal life. I still talk to those fans, but I remember that I'm there to eat dinner, not put on a show.

• • •

But I've also managed to do something even riskier.

This past September, I turned to Gene and told him that I was ready to find my birth father — that I knew he was out there somewhere back in the Ukraine and that I was strong enough to find him. We tried everything — from Red Cross tracing services to the Ukrainian Federation — with no

OKSANA BAIUL · UKRAINE

Oksana Baiul, born in 1977, was three years old when she received her first pair of ice skates from her grandfather. She dreamed of participating in the Olympics, and in 1994, showing tremendous determination, the young Ukrainian woman won the Olympic gold medal. Oksana now lives in the United States and skates with Stars on Ice. She also designs and owns her own clothing line, the Oksana Baiul Collection.

luck. Finally, I decided to just pick up the phone and dial my old skating rink in Dnipropetrovsk, the small town where I grew up. When someone answered on the other end, he identified himself as the director of the skating rink. I was so happy to hear his voice!

I began by introducing myself, "Hi, this is Oksana Baiul . . ." He hung up on me immediately. I called back, and he told me not to play practical jokes. I said, "I swear to you, this is Oksana Baiul." And I started naming all the people I knew in town and what the rink looked like, and finally he believed me.

You would not believe what this guy did for us. He searched from door to door until finally he knocked on the right door, and my father answered. And when we got the news that he had found Sergei Baiul, Gene and I nervously bought tickets to head back to the Ukraine.

My father left my mother and me when I was two. He never remarried. And he still lived in the same house, on the same little quiet street, with my grandmother. Knocking on that door after all these years and seeing him answer was one of the most challenging things I've ever done.

I also went back to my mother's grave for the first time since I was thirteen.

This was the hardest part for me: I was nervous. And I'd been through so much. And I missed her so much.

And then I went back to the skating rink where I had learned to skate. And there were tons of little kids there, surrounding me. They remembered me after all these years and looked up to me. And they grabbed my hands and said, "Oksana, Oksana, come, come, let me show you where we have your picture on the wall." I had spent all those years in the United States feeling lonely, and the whole time there were all these kids who looked up to me. It really put things in perspective.

We're planning to do a charity show for those kids at the skating rink next year. And just a few weeks ago, I got a phone call from my dad, who asked me for my address. I couldn't figure out why he wouldn't just email me a message or call, but then I got a birthday card in the mail from him — the first birthday card since I was two years old. I have my father back.

It's been a roller coaster, but I've learned that no matter what happens, no matter what challenges life brings, you have to just take a few big breaths, believe in yourself, and pick yourself back up. If things are bad and it's hard to be alive . . . well, things will get better. You really just have to believe it. That's all. You have to believe.

There is a higher power, and you can ask for help to get through the tough moments. And most important, you can also reach out to those around you. Surrounding yourself with people whom you love, with a community, is so important. I would never in a million years give up that gold medal. But at the end of the day, our experiences mean so much more when we have people to share them with. For me, it's Gene, it's my father, it's the thought of those kids back at my old skating rink in the Ukraine.

These are the things that sustain me — my roots.

ANI DIFRANCO · USA

Ani DiFranco was born in Buffalo, New York. For her first album, Ani rejected offers from record labels, instead starting her own record company, Righteous Babe Records. She is a punk folksinger who writes songs that simultaneously appeal to old folks and climb the college radio charts. She won the 2003 Grammy Award for Best Recording Package for her album *Evolve*. Ani has recorded and produced more than fourteen popular musical albums.

BELOW Lyrics to "Willing to Fight" from the album *Puddle Dive*

Willing to Fight

The windows of my soul
are made of one-way glass
don't bother looking into my eyes
if there's something you want to know,
just ask
I got a dead bolt stroll
where I'm going is clear
I won't wait for you to wonder
I'll just tell you why I'm here

'cause I know the biggest crime
is just to throw up your hands
say
this has nothing to do with me
I just want to live as comfortably as I can
you got to look outside your eyes
you got to think outside your brain
you got to walk outside your life
to where the neighborhood changes

tell me who is your boogieman
that's who I will be
you don't have to like me for who I am
but we'll see what you're made of
by what you make of me

I think that it's absurd
that you think I
am the derelict daughter
I fight fire with words
words are hotter than flames
words are wetter than water

I got friends all over this country
I got friends in other countries too
I got friends I haven't met yet
I got friends I never knew
I got lovers whose eyes
I've only seen at a glance
I got strangers for great grandchildren
I got strangers for ancestors

I was a long time coming
I'll be a long time gone
You've got your whole life to do something
and that's not very long
so why don't you give me a call
when you're willing to fight
for what you think is real
for what you think is right

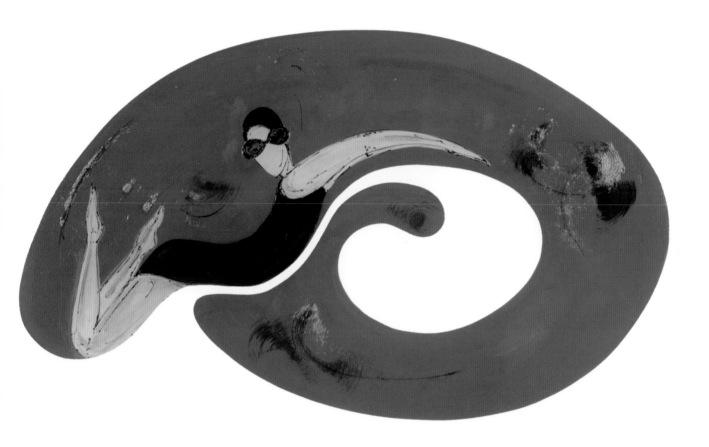

ANDREA ANNUNZIATA • BRAZIL

Andrea Annunziata is from São Paulo and is the daughter of a jewelry designer. She graduated with a degree in architecture and city planning from the faculty of fine arts of Fundação Armando Álvares Penteado (FAAP). In the course of her studies, she developed the concept of incorporating her own mixed-media artwork within architectural design.

ABOVE AND FOLLOWING PAGE *Mulheres Moluscas (Mollusk Women)* series

When we make art, we create dreams. I try to turn people's attention towards this inner, unrevealed world. In my opinion, it's absolutely impossible to help our sick environment without having deeper insight into ourselves.

CAITLIN SISLIN • USA

Caitlin Sislin grew up in the sprawling metropolis of Los Angeles but spent her first few years living in the countryside outside of the city, to which she attributes her dear love of trees, soil, and open sky. She is studying environmental law and hopes to be involved in advocacy related to urban environmental issues and sustainable development.

The nation waits

The nation waits.
Newscasters bring word of the
day's events
each evening to a populace gripped and knotty with anticipation.
High officials throughout the land are seen to confer in tense
   whispers.
Phones ring,
horns honk,
shouts and cries blend into a cacophony of concern
day and night.
No one sleeps.
Even the nation's children lie awake,
sheets tangled,
coursing with energy.
At mealtimes the children watch their parents' shadowed faces,
waiting for change.
Parents wait. Everyone waits.
There is no attempt to conceal the expectation
or even to turn away and find mute comfort in routine.
Gravity seems to crackle with tension,
and the moon's passage to grow erratic.
Then,
one afternoon,
the change comes.

For a moment,
one can detect only the wholeness of silence.
And then, issuing from all the radios and televisions,
spreading from teachers to students,
chefs to waitresses to lunchtime diners,
racing from the bottoms to the tops of all the tall buildings,
comes the news:
the mother Whale has given birth.
In captivity and against all calculated odds,
she has birthed her baby,
bringing the world's Whale population to thirty-two.
Away from zero by one more.
Slowly, the humans begin to celebrate.
Exhaling long laughing breaths,
running out from schoolyard gates,
lifting their glasses to the
fragile abundance of One.
Through the night they sleep and make love deeply
knowing that they are joined
finally
by one more spirit
racing soundlessly beside its mother
into the endless blue-gray deep.

The Dream of Creating a Better Country

"We are the hope, the protagonists, the ones who can turn this long-suffering nation's dream into reality." This is a small part of the hymn of Messengers of Peace (one of my organizations), a hymn we use to tell Colombians and the world what we think.

We strive to make all children and youth aware of the social responsibility of creating peace in our country. Peace does not just refer to an end to problems or to armed conflict, but rather to changing the way that human beings relate — shifting our values and committing to our planet.

The world is spinning, searching for answers. They are destroying my dreams with war and lies. But I said no. I said no to the destruction because Christ took me and showed me the way, and he made me a champion.

I live in a country that is going through a difficult period, and it has wounded us to the core. Little by little, our armed conflict is destroying the essence of our beautiful Colombia. International Humanitarian Law, the only set of rules that can begin to relieve the terrible pain of the people who find themselves in the middle of the conflict, is violated. In our territory there are more than three armed groups fighting each other: the guerillas, the paramilitaries, and the military. Gangs are growing, showing boys the easy way to survive. Child abuse and mistreatment are taking place in every corner of our country.

In 1996 a group of representatives of children and youth from several child-welfare organizations in Colombia met and decided to collaborate in our work with children and youth. Though we were based in different parts of the country, each group was doing incredible work, and we were all striving to help end the Colombian conflict and promote the well-being of children.

We decided to do something on a national scale because our country needed to know what we were working towards. We also decided that the participants themselves should be children. One of the child activists suggested that we stage a vote. But how could we do that when children didn't even have the right to vote?

After a couple of hours of discussion we decided to hold our own election, one specifically for children. We hoped that our election would cause adults to listen to the voice of Colombia's children and recognize our rights, as well as our desire for peace. When we told the adults in our organizations about this plan, the reaction was divided. Some said it was a good idea, and others said that

MAYERLY SÁNCHEZ • COLOMBIA

Mayerly Sánchez is a peace activist and volunteer from Colombia. At the young age of twelve, inspired by the violent death of her close friend Milton, Mayerly established the Colombian Children's Movement for Peace. The movement aims to provide children with the resources to promote nonviolence among their peers. Mayerly and her movement were nominated for the Nobel Peace Prize in 1998.

we were crazy, that we would never accomplish that on a national scale. We joined forces with the adults who believed in us, and we got to work.

The ballot we developed listed twelve of the universal rights established by the Convention on the Rights of Children, which was ratified in Colombia in 1991. Then our mission was to do outreach in elementary and high schools, churches, and other institutions throughout the nation, explaining to everyone under eighteen why it was important to come to the polls and vote responsibly for peace and civil rights, to stop the child abuse.

The big day arrived — October 26, 1996. At first we were a little scared, but then we saw that children, youth, parents, and grandparents were gathering in Colombia's biggest parks, and there were clowns, balloons, and caravans to help promote our cause. That election day was the first day that the media did not portray the presence of any armed group on television or in the papers. It was truly a day of happiness for the country, and especially for the children and youths, because on that day we felt that we were heard.

A total of 2,700 children and youths voted to affirm that the most important rights in Colombia are the rights to life, to peace, to love and family. Through this vote, we taught adults a lesson — that the majority of children and youths think about the common good, not the individual. We showed this by voting for education.

Clearly, we could not stop with the results of the vote, so with the help of other groups we created an assembly. In that assembly we created a minor's code, where we proposed that youths should not be obliged to serve time in the military. Today this is a reality. One year after our vote, more than ten thousand adult Colombians supported our mandate; they voted for peace, life, and liberty, saying with their vote that they would not involve more children and youths in the war, that they would not kidnap people, and that all of Colombia should be allowed to live in peace.

All the participants in the Colombian Children's Movement for Peace were committed to our country, and we were the ones going into schools and teaching children and youths how to claim their rights without letting their responsibilities fall to the wayside. We held daily trainings and formed a solid base, mostly using games as teaching tools.

World Vision Colombia, one institution I am a part of, supported us and understood that we

continued

wanted to have our own space to do our work in. That's why after years of work in community projects, we created Messengers of Peace, a space where children, youths, and adults could make possible the construction of a culture of peace. In this organization the participation of children and youths is essential to the process of development in a community with scarce resources. This whole experience was strengthened by the participation and active involvement of youth in all stages of planning, execution, and follow-through on national and regional levels, and in program development in different cities.

Our mission is for young people to exercise their citizenship around the building of peace and democratic bases. In doing this, we achieve the recognition that we are legitimate players in society. In the movement's own process, we seek to promote the recognition and application of the Convention on the Rights of Children (emphasizing articles 12–15, 17, and 30–31, which have to do with participation) and our national constitution (which speaks about the rights of children and adolescents in articles 44–45, 50, and 67).

Children and youths from the movement dream of being the protagonists in building a culture of peace in Colombia, of taking on an active role that is purposeful and responsible in different areas of civil society and government, calling on Christian values as central to our mission.

This protagonism is represented by our desire to actively contribute to the construction of peace in our country, starting with our own lives, those of our families, and those of the communities where we live.

Our biggest achievement to date is visible in the thousands of hopeful smiles on the faces of the children and youths that we are training; they now know it is possible to dream and change the world. The best way to bring about change, and the most basic, is to be active in your community — to work, play, and learn with your neighbors, identifying problems and coming up with helpful solutions together.

I think that the most important mission for all of humanity, and especially for me, is to follow Jesus Christ and be his instrument of peace on earth, helping the less fortunate and showing them that opportunities exist in the world. I hope each of us will be an instrument that, with love and leadership, accompanies human beings who have lost hope.

I am sure that you can see a change in this generation because the world vision of youth is to cast away the constraints that society imposes. We are showing this awareness and looking for ways to develop the skills we have learned in childhood and adolescence to make positive changes in our country and in the world.

In this way, we as women play an important role. We are the ones in charge of making life a little sweeter because we are sensitive, loving, and respectful of the problems that afflict humans, especially children and youth. The female members of the Messengers of Peace movement define ourselves by the ways in which we have searched for a space to participate in society, a space where we can exercise our citizenship and play a part in searching for solutions to the problems we all face, by means of nonviolent intervention. That is something that we are planting in the hearts of all human beings whom we meet.

[FROM THE ORIGINAL SPANISH]

"Somos la esperanza, los protagonistas, realizando el sueño de esta nación que tanto ha sufrido." Este es un pequeño fragmento del himno de Gestores de Paz donde les decimos a los colombianos y al mundo, lo que pensamos.

Touch Wood	Tatchédogbé
I woke up	Umbe nafon-eh
today	Wa un'g kwo
feeling	Ta ra-tach'robe
good	Yeman kokuah
touch wood	Nunawa'ha
and thank heavens	Ena wanio
As long as	Oh-k`hohe
I'm breathing	R'okane yem-mieba
anything	Oh-kw'ha h'ungkwo
is possible	Tah-romok'aneware
In the same house	Kwe gwe'ng djare ka-ka
that a child	Oh kwe ro-kwe-kwe
dies	Tche'ha nonide
A new child	Oh nudakwe-oh tcho
will flourish	Do sa kwassila

[FROM THE ORIGINAL FON]

ANGÉLIQUE KIDJO • BENIN

Angélique Kidjo was born in 1960 in Benin, West Africa. As a young adult, she relocated to Paris. She speaks (and sings in) eight languages, and her music emphasizes cultural connections by weaving together rhythms from her native country with musical styles from around the globe. Angélique believes children embody ourl hope for the future, and she has been a UNICEF Goodwill Ambassador since 2002.

ABOVE Lyrics to "Tatchédogbé" (Touch Wood) from the album *Ayé*

I continue to be inspired, to be filled with admiration and awed, by the abundance of feminine myths and tales that I have discovered about seeds, plants, and food, and by cultural and biological diversity itself. My paintings are not only a personal channel to express the intimate sense of nature that I deeply identify with, but also a bridge to communicate, transmit, and educate others about the message of traditional wisdom.

VALENTINA CAMPOS · BOLIVIA

Valentina Campos is a third-generation Bolivian artist. As a mother and an activist, she works to protect and strengthen traditional culture and the environment through dialogue, education, art, and other activities. Painting is her preferred medium for conveying her experience and knowledge. She lives in Cochabamba with her husband and son.

RIGHT *Mamela Mauka* (from the *Mamalas* series)

Without a doubt, my generation is defined by the need for freedom and self-determination for women, especially in Africa, where there is still a lot of work to do in terms of integrating women into the processes of globalization and technological advancement.

[FROM THE ORIGINAL FRENCH]

Ma génération se définit sans aucun doute par le besoin de liberté et d'émancipation des femmes, notamment en Afrique où il y a encore beaucoup de travail à faire pour intégrer les femmes dans le processus de mondialisation et des nouvelles technologies.

PATRICIA DJOMSEU • CAMEROON / FRANCE

Patricia Djomseu heads an industrial engineering and manufacturing company and serves as the president of Women of Africa, a nonprofit organization that works to better standards of living for women on her home continent. In her photography Patricia addresses black women's sexual freedom, such as the freedom to choose a partner of the same sex. She resides in France and the United States.

RIGHT *Black Women Today*

ANA MARÍA GARCÍA MORENO • COLOMBIA

Ana María García Moreno is a graphic designer and photographer who lives in Bogotá. She is deeply religious, having become a devout Christian in her adult life. Through her work, she addresses ethnic and cultural diversity, along with the differing aesthetic and corporal values that change and develop according to race and over time.

BELOW *Solidaridad (Solidarity)*

I see women as an overarching force. There is validity in the diversity of archetypes, in the contrasts among them.

It seems to me that the most important change we can effect as a generation is to reflect on our creative powers, so that people will look at and think about the many different things that are full of hope, light, and life. I would love to leave a legacy that touches people's souls and makes them understand that racial, ideological, geographic, and economic differences are cultural in nature and invented by human beings.

PANHAVUT CHIM • CAMBODIA

Panhavut Chim was born in 1982, but her parents changed her birth year on her birth certificate to 1981 so she could attend school earlier. Panhavut has worked for various international nongovernmental organizations (NGOs) and hopes to fulfill her dream of traveling the world.

Imagine Freedom

Floating on the surface of water, I imagined I was a boat that could travel freely to any destination in the world. As I dropped my body into the water, I held my breath and tried hard to use my feet and my hands to keep myself from submerging. I wore goggles, so I could see the beam illuminating the water. It appeared like a crystal-clear glass enabling me to see everything deeply. Oblivious to the men who were swimming in the same pool, other young Cambodian women were happily learning to swim, just as I was. We were more courageous than the older generation, who lived in the city where there was no pool.

Ever since I first opened my eyes to the sunlight, I have never had the privilege of meeting or knowing my grandfathers and three of my siblings because they died from starvation during the Pol Pot regime. As a child I usually stayed with my grandma, my father's mother, and she told me stories — stories about her, stories about my parents, and stories about me when I was younger. She once told me my mother didn't produce enough milk for me when I was born in 1982 because she was weak after the brutal regime. Unfortunately, I couldn't drink powered milk due to an aversion to particular types of food; I always threw up or had diarrhea if I drank it. Hence, I was breastfed by other ladies who had just given birth.

My father was a teacher and my mother was a nurse before the regime, and after it ended, they had to start their lives again — with only ten chi of gold that my grandma had kept for them while they were separated from each other.

The aftermath of genocide left my country with many widows and orphans. One of my aunts left her two children while she visited her aunt in Paris before the regime, but she was then refused entry back into the country. About ten years later, she finally found her children: one was living with an old man, and another was a monk at a pagoda in the same village in Takeo province.

After completing high school in 1997, I continued to study for a bachelor of arts degree, relying on my parents' support. "It's auspicious for your generation to have a chance to study more, so work hard for your education and your brighter future," said my grandma. "I never had the opportunity to attend any school. However, I gave birth to children with a desire for knowledge, such as your father."

One day, when I was a freshman at the university, my mom entered my room and told me that one of my relatives wanted to marry me. She described his positive characteristics: he was a good man, polite, responsible, suave, generous, and friendly. I knew him because he had been my English teacher when I was thirteen; that was his part-time job in addition to his full-time job at an international NGO (World Vision) in Phnom Penh. I believed that he was a good man. He was about ten years older than I was. I didn't say much to my mom but to reply,

continued

"I have no idea, Mom. Everything is up to you and Daddy. But let me finish my studies first." The man and his family agreed to wait for me. My parents were understanding; they didn't force me to do anything, and they didn't decide anything for me without my acknowledgment. This differs from old times when parents could force their children to obey their will. There are still some Cambodian families that follow that out-of-date custom. Usually they don't let their children study much, especially daughters.

While I was undertaking my second year at university, I found a part-time job as an interviewer for a marketing research company. There I gained some experience with the different natures of people. For the first time I felt weary because I had to travel from one district to another to interview product consumers. Happiness came to me when my tasks were completely finished.

The more I became exposed to everyday life and had the opportunity to meet new and interesting people through my working environment, the more I began to appreciate the importance of social activities and a meaningful life. A thought continually nagged at my subconscious: "You're not civilized!" I asked myself what a savage life was. I came to a stronger understanding of myself and other Cambodian women. Women traditionally chose to stay at home, get married, and look after their children and family. They were not well educated, and men determined that women were housekeepers whose ideas were not accepted or important.

During my studies at the university, some of my friends got married, and some of them became mothers and stopped studying in order to stay at home and raise a family. A prejudiced fear possessed me again that the same fate could befall me and I would be forced to cancel my studies. I had already decided that I wanted to study for an MBA when I finished my BA. Despite the pressures of tradition, a magical strength consumed me to be open-minded and to defeat all the constraints I was facing in order to reach my goal. I then made up my mind again about the upcoming marriage that my mom had asked me to consider. In a fit of blind bravado, I asked my mom to inform my fiancé and his family to not wait for me and to think about finding someone who would be a more suitable companion. A year later, my mom informed me that the man was going to marry a lady who was older than I was.

Later on, after I graduated with my BA, I acquired a full-time job at a private company where I studied multifariously about a new society. "It's not easy for a woman to travel to anywhere like a man," my mom once said. "Once you have a family and children, you need to be responsible. So if you choose to travel, you will not have enough time to take care of them. It's better to stay with your family. However, I don't forbid you to walk on your track. We will still support you, although you're old enough to manage your own life. We have only you — our sole daughter — and we do everything just for you." At that time, a glimpse of my human ego was reflected as I tried to deeply digest the dreams she had for me. I understand that everything I do, I do for my family and the world.

As I pulled myself up from the water, my spirit came back to me, and I awoke from the dream by telling myself, "This is the real world you're facing." I looked around and saw my American friend Rachael, who works for another NGO as a missionary, staring at me from the other side of the pool. She cried, "You did it well." I continued swimming towards where she was, thinking, "Life is meaningless unless the light of fulfillment inside you rises up. Imagine all you can, for it's all you can do."

PHILLIPPA YAA DE VILLIERS-VENTER • SOUTH AFRICA

Phillippa Yaa de Villiers-Venter is a South African writer, performer, and poet living in Johannesburg. She studied journalism in South Africa and theater in Paris and then returned to academia in the late 1990s, consolidating her passions for writing and performance with a degree in dramatic arts. She writes for a television series in South Africa. In this poem, she writes of the Hillbrow Tower, the tallest building in Johannesburg.

The River

One day the Hillbrow Tower started to cry.
Real tears poured down its sides,
collected in the gutters, and ran down Banket Street,
and when
the other buildings saw the tower's sadness
they started to weep in sympathy.
Soon the whole city was sobbing,
the tears joined other tears
and filled the depressions and valleys.
They covered the koppies,
and collected in City Deep
Cascading over Gold Reef City
Flooding Fordsburg
And soaking Soweto.
They flowed until they became a river
That carried us into the night,
Where our dreams grew taller than buildings
Taller than buildings

Arab women today have many rights. We make considerable and vital decisions in our own lives and in our society in general. We are becoming more aware and independent every day. This awareness makes us more sensitive to other women's difficulties, to our responsibilities, and to the problems that are increasing day by day.

Greater challenges and responsibilities are loaded on our women, but they give them much experience. I see and respect how concepts like belief, career, education, and family hold great presence in the lives of the women of my generation. On the other hand, I also feel content when I see an uneducated woman running her house and her own simple business perfectly, under very difficult life conditions. Such a woman reflects how naturally strong and talented women are.

I consider myself an open-minded woman who respects the differences between us all, but I still aim for a more "habitable" future. I have been a lucky person, mingling throughout my life with diverse cultures and people and getting really close to the point where differences evaporate.

My artistic aim is to highlight the gender issue, not from a feminist point of view but from the position of a female with a personal understanding of herself and others and the skill and ability to represent her experiences. I link women's concerns, thoughts, fears, lack of love, abuse, and the cycle of a woman's fertility to issues such as globalization, heritage, and identity.

PERIHAN ABOU ZIED • EGYPT

Perihan Abou Zied was born in 1978 in Egypt. Her multicultural upbringing away from her country had a deep impact on her character and artistic development, giving her the spontaneity and open-minded approach that she brings to her life and her work.

ABOVE *Karima* **RIGHT** *Gazing;* both pieces from the *Al Kourouj (Opening Up)* series

I am from Senegal, I am thirty-two years old, and I am the mother of two little girls. I am Muslim and one of those multifaceted visual artists. I live in Dakar, the capital of Senegal, and I am a pure product of this new generation: a generation of professionals, of career-driven and family-driven young women. We are great lovers of nature, spiritual vibrations, and developing our nation.

FATOU KANDÉ SENGHOR • SENEGAL

Fatou Kandé Senghor is a visual artist, documentary filmmaker, and educator. She studied in France and has traveled extensively in Africa and Europe. She cofounded the Waru Studio as a platform for dialogue for filmmakers of her generation to explore new technologies as an alternative to the dying film industry and a voice to the peoples of her rich and misunderstood continent, Africa. She has written in numerous publications about the African experience in film and about gender issues in the African context. She lives in Dakar with her two daughters, Oumy-Dior and Safiétou-Salane.

ABOVE *Sans title (Untitled)*

LORENA OCHOA • MEXICO

Named best golfer in Mexico from 1997 to 2000, Lorena Ochoa is Mexico's most popular female athlete, an eight-time national champion, and the youngest person ever to earn the National Sports Award, which she received in 2000 from President Vicente Fox. As a child, she would go hiking, camping, and horseback riding with her family around their retreat in Tapalpa, which lies west of Guadalajara, where Lorena was born in 1981.

More Than I Ever Imagined

More than anything, I want to say that being an athlete and representing my country is an honor for me. I am very proud of being Mexican. Every time I play I have the colors of the Mexican flag in my heart. I play for myself, my parents, my friends, and my whole country. Being a model for others is a big responsibility, but I take on that responsibility with a lot of joy. This is why I always try to do things in the right way, so kids can follow in my footsteps, so they can dream of doing the same thing someday. I thank God for giving me this opportunity.

As an athlete I am 100 percent certain that mistakes and losses teach you more than anything — both in sports and in life. I learn how to win and work harder because I don't like the feeling of losing. I believe this is where I get my motivation and courage to keep practicing harder and harder, to never give up. You learn to love the game and the feeling of competition. You learn how to be a champion. You do whatever it takes to become one, and if that means making sacrifices, well — you do it.

I think my generation has more opportunities than my mother's generation. So my advice is to not be afraid of dreaming and going far. If you look for opportunities, you will find them. In my life right now, I have much more than I ever imagined I could have, and this is simply because I never stop dreaming.

A lot of kids these days are worried about what other people think of them, and most kids are even afraid to say what they think. I believe being someone different is something very good. We need unique people. Unique people know how to take the lead, and they will always be remembered.

I am sure that the next generation of women is going to be better in many different ways. In the world of sports, women's participation is growing quickly, and I am happy to be part of that. Little by little, women are getting the attention and place they deserve. For me, being a woman is the best present I received from God. And I thank Him every day for what I have.

As a generation of women, we have limitless possibilities, and we should all learn to map our journey and identify these possibilities. Once we have made achievements as individuals, it will dawn on us that we are all one large, beautiful quilt, made of individual stitches. Stitches represent unhurried action. Our journey into the future should be unhurried; it should be one of perseverance, dedication, and love. As we move forward, we should embrace one another and have an underlying understanding of the spirit of sisterhood.

We are branches borne of strong trees. These branches have no boundaries. We float in the sky, taking in the breeze and the sunshine. We, the branches, are able to reach far and wide.

NAOMI WANJIKU • KENYA

Naomi Wanjiku has worked with fibers and fabrics ever since she was a child. Her grandmother's friends were basket weavers, and from them she learned to use the local materials to make *migiyo* (fibers, in the Kĩkũyũ language). She received formal art and design training at the University of Nairobi and the University of California, Los Angeles, where she did her graduate work.

LEFT *Two Trees and Branches*

I paint hands, I paint the human body, I paint different aspects of women. I capture the Latin woman, not submissive and sad but strong and contemporary, in image and idea.

In my work I include many subjects that worry me, so that it makes those who see my paintings think. I do not try to be an activist or a protest painter. But on the day that my future children ask me about how we left the world in their hands, about the contamination, the wars, the corruption, et cetera, I do not want to have to respond, "I did not do anything."

LORENA RODRÍGUEZ • MEXICO

Lorena Rodríguez, the daughter of painter and art professor Elsa Ayala, was born in Monterrey, Mexico, in 1972. Painting has always been an integral part of her life. In her work, she seeks to break stereotypes of Latin women as suffering and self-sacrificing and instead portrays them as strong and modern.

RIGHT *Metamorfosis (Metamorphosis)*

Edge of the Earth

Some of us with the luck of the draw — born in the most auspicious place at the most auspicious time, and then fueled for any number of reasons — make that journey to the edge and poke our heads out into space. We look into territory previously uncharted by any in our sisterhood, gather courage as a cloak around our shoulders, trembling with fear or anticipation, and breathe deeply before taking the plunge.

Behind are others whose lives are still steeped in traditions and old ways of doing things. Others who adjust and adjust to changes that come and who yet believe that change is something that happens to them and not something that they can cause. For them, the immutability of things is its own good news.

And between those of us at the edge and those of us at the center is a cord that binds. A cord that we feel in both places. At the center, it is as an amorphous wondering: Might something else not be possible, or is this always all there is? And at the edge, it is a bittersweet realization: Life could have been easier than this. If only we could have closed our eyes more, demanded less, accepted less, been less. Some say you can only be who you are, but in our hearts we recall, if vaguely, the choices that brought us onto roads less traveled, which for want of traffic become narrow paths, then trails, until all that remains is wilderness.

Far off in the distance, we hear a sound. It is only the wind. Or it might be a message from those who have ventured this far before. The wind might bear their wisdom to us. Except that we don't understand; there is no one among us who can interpret. Or if there are interpreters, we might not know of them.

At the edge there is little talking. Soon we realize that the edge is also harsh. It is a world with too many questions without answers; it entails living with the void that remains when all beliefs are taken away. Silence becomes an armor here. And our eyes focus on some distant place, or it may just be that we look there to avoid looking here, where the mess of uncertainty gathers at our feet.

At the center, our eyes are quiet and clear. They look warm and sweet. Here sisters hold hands, and during long walks to waters that move farther away, we sing. The sick find the small hollows of our hands, brimming with water, against their lips. Soon, their sickly forms fill with our giving and our stories. With transitions, our keening connects the

HAFSAT ABIOLA • NIGERIA

For Hafsat's bio and photo, please see page 127.

skies and the mother earth. Yet the center makes never-ending demands for our labor, so that from dawn to dusk we work, tending to everyone but ourselves.

At the edge, we begin to see that we ought to have brought our roots with us. But when we set off, baggage seemed tiresome and was left behind. So here we stand, perilously at the border, with the wind about our ears and our feet shaky on the ground.

What joy is the cord that links us all. The cord that connects our sisterhood across distances, time zones, worlds also connects the different aspects of who we are. So that even as each of us is an embodiment of contradictions, the center holds all the pieces together. We don't fall apart. Or if we do, it is possible to pick all the pieces up again. It is even possible to arrange them in a new design. This cord now brings us back to the lands we've known. From the edge, ours are the eyes filled with mystery. And from the center, ours are the feet rooted into the soil of time and place.

And now we come together.

Bringing together what we have seen, who we have been, as we weave new patterns,

streaking the land with our magic.

RESOURCES FOR ACTION

Chances are if you're reading this, you've got a lot of resources at your fingertips — maybe even more than you think. You're probably educated, so you could write a decent letter to a newspaper or magazine editor or government official on behalf of your peers. You're likely to have Internet access, so you could easily look up any of the thousands of organizations working on behalf of women globally and join their mailing list. You (or someone who loves you) shelled out a good amount of pocket change for this book, so you could find at least that amount to donate to a nonprofit organization working to improve the lives of women. (By the way, if you've never done that, try it! It's an amazing feeling to put your money where your mouth is.)

Here we've picked just a few issues affecting the well-being of women around the world — some of which affect our generation disproportionately and many of which cut across generations. It goes without saying that there are infinite ways for you to make an impact, so if you're not inspired by our suggestions, by all means, come up with your own!

What we highlight here is only the tip of the iceberg. If you want more depth, visit our website (www.imow.org), and be sure to check out the Imagining Ourselves Online Exhibit and Global Gathering between March 8 and June 30, 2006. You'll find many more suggestions and coverage of more issues than we have room for here.

Let us know what you're up to, and perhaps most important, have fun! Imagine: millions of young women in their twenties and thirties, getting out there, going to bat for each other — and laughing and telling crazy jokes and stories to each other and just having an awesome time while doing it. Yes, this is serious stuff, but working on it can be some of the most fun you'll ever experience.

HIV/AIDS

Known in the 1980s as a "gay white man's" disease, HIV/AIDS is now a global health epidemic that disproportionately affects women — and especially young women in their reproductive years. In many parts of the world, women and girls are not as likely to be able to refuse unwanted or unprotected sex and are therefore more likely to become victims. In South Africa, 20 to 48 percent of young girls report that their first sexual experience was forced, according to the South African Humanitarian Information Network.[1] It is perhaps not a coincidence that a whopping 77 percent of South Africa's HIV-positive youth population is female.[2]

Around the world, young women are organizing health campaigns, giving community talks, designing and distributing posters and brochures for their peers, and working in local clinics serving HIV/AIDS clients. Their knowledge is the key to an HIV/AIDS–free future for themselves and for their communities. You could join them!

To learn more or get involved, check out:

> UNAIDS: www.unaids.org

> STAYING ALIVE: eu.staying-alive.org

> PATHFINDER INTERNATIONAL: www.pathfind.org

> YOUTH NET: www.fhi.org/en/youth/youthnet/index.htm

> AFRICA ALIVE AND LOVE LIFE (in Africa): www.africaalive.org, www.lovelife.ch/stopaids.php

> ENTRA EN ACCIÓN (in Latin America): www.EntraenAccion.org

TRAFFICKING OF YOUNG WOMEN

Worldwide, it is estimated that more than 700,000 women and girls are trafficked every year.[3] In some countries, the sex trade has become a development strategy and a source of income whose profits amount to 14 percent of the gross domestic product (GDP).[4] In the United States and elsewhere, the vast majority of international (80 percent) and U.S. (83 percent) women involved in the sex trade entered the sex industry before the age of twenty-five, many of them as children.[5]

Young women are particularly vulnerable to the traffic rings offering work or marriage abroad. These women are often without hope for a future in their own country and filled with dreams of a better life in countries such as Italy, Germany, England, Bosnia, or the United States. Young girls accepting these offers often find themselves in brothels, illegal bars, or private homes where they are beaten and abused into submission. Many are forced to be sex slaves for their captors, and some are forced to work as domestic slaves.

To learn more or get involved, check out:

> COALITION TO ABOLISH SLAVERY AND TRAFFICKING: www.castla.org

> POLARIS PROJECT: www.polarisproject.org

> FAIR FUND: www.fairfund.org

> EQUALITY NOW: www.equalitynow.org

> INTERNATIONAL ORGANIZATION FOR MIGRATION: www.iom.int

> INTERNATIONAL ORGANIZATION FOR ADOLESCENTS: www.iofa.org

DOMESTIC VIOLENCE

Domestic violence affects women and girls in every corner of the globe in terrifying proportions. It cuts across race, religion, income, class, and culture. Globally, at least one in three women and girls has been beaten or sexually abused in her lifetime, most often at the hands of someone she knows.[6] According to the United Nations Population Fund, women between the ages of fifteen and forty-four lose more discounted health years of life (DHYLs) to rape and domestic violence than to breast cancer, cervical cancer, obstructed labor, heart disease, AIDS, respiratory infections, motor vehicle accidents, or war.[7]

To learn more or get involved, check out:

> AMNESTY INTERNATIONAL, VIOLENCE AGAINST WOMEN FACT SHEET: www.amnestyusa.org/stopviolence/factsheets/violence.html

> AMNESTY INTERNATIONAL'S WOMEN'S HUMAN RIGHTS ACTIONS: www.amnestyusa.org/women/index.do

> WORLD HEALTH ORGANIZATION'S INFORMATION ON GENDER-BASED VIOLENCE (in French, Spanish, and English): www.who.int/gender/violence/en

> ANTI-VIOLENCE RESOURCE GUIDE, including a Global Guide: www.feminist.com/antiviolence

> V-DAY: www.vday.org/main.html

> THE 1% CAMPAIGN TO BRING ABOUT A WORLD WITHOUT VIOLENCE: www.vday.org/onepercent (coordinated by V-Day and the National Organization for Women [NOW]).

WOMEN AND POLITICS

Despite major recent advances of women in politics around the world, women in positions of political leadership are still a rarity. In 2005, women comprise only 16 percent of political representatives around the world.[8] Out of 192 countries, only nine have female heads of state or government, and only five have a female vice president.[9] Young women in their twenties and thirties today, many of whom have benefited from increased education, are in an ideal position to strive to improve these figures. There are a number of ways to make a difference, whether it's registering your friends to vote, supporting women's political leadership training, or even running for office yourself.

To learn more or get involved, check out:

> THE INTERNATIONAL INSTITUTE FOR DEMOCRACY AND ELECTORAL ASSISTANCE (IDEA) GENDER AND POLITICAL PARTICIPATION PROJECT: www.idea.int/gender

> GLOBAL DATABASE OF QUOTAS FOR WOMEN, A JOINT PROJECT OF IDEA AND STOCKHOLM UNIVERSITY, SWEDEN: www.quotaproject.org

> WOMEN'S LEARNING PARTNERSHIP FOR RIGHTS, DEVELOPMENT, AND PEACE (WLP): www.learningpartnership.org/facts/leadership.phtml

> CENTER FOR ASIA-PACIFIC WOMEN IN POLITICS: www.capwip.org

> EUROPEAN WOMEN'S LOBBY: www.womenlobby.org

> PROLEAD: WOMEN LEADERS BUILDING THE FUTURE IN LATIN AMERICA AND THE CARIBBEAN: www.iadb.org/sds/prolead

> VITAL VOICES GLOBAL PARTNERSHIP: www.vitalvoices.org

> THE WHITE HOUSE PROJECT (U.S.-BASED): www.thewhitehouseproject.org

REPRODUCTIVE HEALTH

Reproductive health care saves lives. Across the globe, women and girls die every minute from complications in pregnancy or childbirth, resulting in more than half a million deaths per year. And for each maternal fatality, another twenty women become ill or permanently disabled.[10] Most of these dire outcomes, almost all of which occur in developing countries, could be prevented with skilled medical care or increased access to reproductive health education and resources. Globally, many young women also fail to get tested for reproductive cancers and sexually transmitted diseases or do not receive adequate prenatal and postnatal care.

While many organizations promote family planning and others promote abstinence, it is clear that lack of access to reproductive health resources is one of the biggest problems facing young adult women today. Making sure that you and your friends and family get annual exams is an important first step towards solving the problem.

To learn more or get involved, check out:

> UNITED NATIONS POPULATION FUND (in Arabic, English, French, and Spanish): www.unfpa.org

> INTERNATIONAL PLANNED PARENTHOOD FEDERATION: www.ippf.org

> TEENWIRE (Planned Parenthood's adolescent health site; in English and Spanish): www.teenwire.com

> ABSTINENCE CLEARINGHOUSE: www.abstinence.net

> SIECUS (SEXUALITY INFORMATION AND EDUCATION COUNCIL OF THE UNITED STATES) DIRECTORY OF INTERNATIONAL REPRODUCTIVE HEALTH ORGANIZATIONS: www.siecus.org/inter/directory/dire0000.html or by topic: www.siecus.org/links/links.html

ECONOMIC EMPOWERMENT

While our generation has entered the workforce in record numbers, there is still a long way to go. According to the International Labour Organization, worldwide, women on average earn two-thirds of what men earn. Seventy percent of the world's 1.3 billion poor — those who are living on the equivalent of less than US $1 per day — are women. Women spend twice as much or more time as men doing unpaid work. Women also make up the majority of the world's part-time workers — between 60 percent and 90 percent.[11]

A variety of strategies have been employed to promote women's equal participation in the economy. Microcredit lending, or small loans for women entrepreneurs, has proven an effective way to increase access to financial resources for women at the local level. In addition, many women have created thriving professional networks to increase the access to resources for participating in business.

To learn more or get involved, check out:

> PRO-MUJER (Latin America): www.promujer.org

> GRAMEEN FOUNDATION: www.grameenfoundation.org

> COUNCIL FOR ECONOMIC EMPOWERMENT FOR WOMEN IN AFRICA: www.ceewauwires.org

> WOMEN'S ENTREPRENEURSHIP PORTAL (European Union): europa .eu.int/comm/enterprise/entrepreneurship/craft/craft-women/womenentr _portal.htm

> ECONOMIC SECURITY PROGRAM, MS. FOUNDATION FOR WOMEN: www.ms.foundation.org

GENERAL RESOURCES

> INTERNATIONAL MUSEUM OF WOMEN: www.imow.org

> GLOBAL FUND FOR WOMEN: www.globalfundforwomen.org

> UNITED NATIONS DEVELOPMENT FUND FOR WOMEN: www.unifem.org

> ASSOCIATION FOR WOMEN'S RIGHTS IN DEVELOPMENT: www.awid.org

> AFRICAN WOMEN'S DEVELOPMENT FUND: www.awdf.org

> MAMA CASH: www.mamacash.nl/english

> WOMEN FOR WOMEN INTERNATIONAL: www.womenforwomen.org